Introduction

What caused the housing bubble that precipitated the 2008 financial crisis? Answers generally fall into one of two categories: those that assign responsibility to an unregulated free market, and those that point to government intervention in the market as itself being the problem. Proponents of the former view argue that the government should regulate and manage the economy, while proponents of the latter argue in favor of a free market. If a solution to the crisis is to be found, it must be based on a correct understanding of its primary causes. Thus, the question of how we are to know which view is the correct is crucial.

This book examines the records of two prominent individuals who have offered diagnoses and prescriptions. Congressmen and presidential candidate Ron Paul has perhaps become the most well-known advocate of the view that it was a government-created crisis and that what is needed is a free market. Nobel-prize winning economist and *New York Times* columnist Paul Krugman has been a prominent advocate of the opposing view that an unregulated free market was the cause and thus that greater government management of the economy is needed. Who is correct?

The question goes beyond the opinions of two individuals. It is really a question about two schools of economic thought. Ron Paul represents the Austrian school, whose luminaries include Ludwig von Mises, Henry Hazlitt, Friedrich A. Hayek, and Murray N. Rothbard, among others, while Paul Krugman represents the Keynesian school, which embraces the theories of British economist John Maynard Keynes. While the Keynesian school advocates that the government should manage the economy, the Austrian school advocates just the opposite: that government interference only creates more problems than it is ostensibly intended to solve. The most important contribution of the Austrian school to the field of economics is its theory of the business cycle, which is unique in offering a comprehensive and coherent explanation for why the economy goes through regular cycles of booms and busts.

So which school has offered a better diagnosis of the causes of the 2008 financial crisis and a better prescription for what to do about it? There is some ancient wisdom that can help to answer this question. The Bible is full of stories about the prophets, the political and economic analysts of their day, and offers a simple answer to the question of how one is to tell the true from the false prophets: those whose predictions come to pass are the true prophets, while those whose predictions do not, the false. There is also a consistent theme that the true prophets issued disturbing warnings that people generally didn't want to here and were thus widely disdained, while the false prophets offered more reassuring messages about what the future had in store and thus were widely celebrated.

The purpose of this book is to review the records of Ron Paul and Paul Krugman on the question of the housing bubble. Who correctly predicted it? Who has offered the more reasonable explanation as to its cause? Who has offered the more sensible response to the bursting of the housing bubble and the financial crisis it precipitated? Most importantly, whose admonitions should we now be regarding as we move into the future? In short, who is the true prophet, and who the false?

Ron Paul vs. Paul Krugman
Austrian vs. Keynesian economics in the
financial crisis

Jeremy R. Hammond

Copyright © 2012 by Jeremy R. Hammond
All rights reserved.
ISBN-10: 1470070723
ISBN-13: 978-1470070724

Contents

Introduction 5
The Dot-Com Bubble 7
The Housing Bubble 15
Crisis and Response 43
Know them by their fruits... 53
Conclusion 63
Appendix: Warnings for the Future 65
About the Author 87
Notes 89
Index 101

The Dot-Com Bubble

In 1997, Congressman Ron Paul warned that the government's policy of subsidizing housing, such as through the Housing and Urban Development (HUD) Agency, was causing a misallocation of resources that was distorting the market.[1] He spoke out against the "transfer of wealth to government housing programs", arguing that it wasn't the poor but the wealthy who benefited most. "It is the rich beneficiaries, those who receive the rents and those who get to build the buildings [who] are the most concerned that this government housing program continues." He also decried the Federal Reserve monetary system that "hurts the poor more than the rich".[2]

Elaborating on the role of the Federal Reserve (or "the Fed"), he warned against the government-enforced monopoly that it had over the supply of money and credit in the United States. "If we are concerned about repealing the business cycle," he said, "we would have to finally understand the Federal Reserve and how they contribute to the business cycle." The Fed's "authority to manipulate interest rates" was "an ominous power" that caused the business cycle and was incompatible with the principle of a free market economy. Its means of doing so was an increase in the money supply, or inflation, which robbed the people of the purchasing power of their dollars. "In a free market," he explained, "interest rates would be determined by savings.... If savings are high, interest rates go down; people then are encouraged to borrow and invest and build businesses."

The Fed's manipulation of the interest rate sent wrong signals to borrowers and investors that created artificial booms. The Fed, he said, "comes along and they crank out the credit and they lower the interest rates artificially, which then encourages business people and consumers

7

to do things that they would not otherwise do. This is the expansion or the bubble part of the business cycle, which then sets the stage for the next recession." But rather than understanding the business cycle and preventing artificial booms, economists and members of Congress were instead vainly focused on preventing the busts by applying more of the same policies that had created the bubble in the first place, thus setting the stage for the next, even greater, recession.[3]

While Ron Paul was expressing these views on the Fed, Paul Krugman was arguing virtually the opposite. He also wrote in his column in the *New York Times* on August 30, 1998 that the "current craziness in world financial markets" could translate into "a global slump", but the cause in his view would be governments *raising* interest rates, rather than having kept them artificially low for too long. He acknowledged that stock prices in the U.S. had been driven to "hard-to-justify heights", but assured that the "real risk to the world economy comes not from bad fundamentals but from rigid ideologies", such as "the belief that a strong currency means a strong economy, that stable prices insure prosperity." In other words, the U.S. economy was fundamentally sound, and all that needed to be done to keep it that way was to inflate to keep interest rates low. "In the end," he wrote, "a global slump is quite an easy thing to prevent."[4]

Ron Paul continued to warn against inflation, stating in September 1998 that the "worldwide financial crisis" then underway was a consequence of operating "with a fiat monetary system" that "has allowed the financial bubble to develop. Easy credit and artificially low interest rates starts a chain reaction that, by its very nature, guarantees a future correction." The "boom part of the cycle lasts for unpredictable lengths of time", but must be followed by a corrective bust. "Fiat money and its low interest rates cause malinvestment, over capacity, rising prices in one industry or another, excessive debt and over-speculation worldwide." Furthermore, "Capitalism erroneously is being blamed. No mention is made that no country today is truly capitalist in following a sound monetary policy." Government bailouts also compounded the problem, encouraging mismanagement of the economy.[5]

He commented further that "the largest of all bubbles is now bursting", reiterating that while "the stimulative effect" of having "central banks generously create credit out of thin air" was "welcomed and applauded as the boom part of the cycle", the "illusions of wealth brought about by artificial wealth creation end when the predictable correction arrives." The trouble was not limited to the U.S. "All countries of the world have participated in this massive inflationary bubble with the dollar leading the way" in its role as the world's reserve currency. He again warned against the Federal Reserve artificially lowering interest rates in response to the financial crisis.[6]

When the Chairman of the Federal Reserve, Alan Greenspan, announced that the Fed would follow the course advocated by Paul Krugman and lower interest rates, Ron Paul responded by saying that the Fed's monetary policy, along with the longstanding government policy of bailing out troubled institutions, would "make the problems much worse."[7] He repeated that the "previous boom supported by the illusion of wealth coming from money creation is the cause of current world events". He said that the resulting bust "cannot be prevented" and attempting to do so would only "prolong the agony". He observed that "Price fixing of interest rates contradicts the basic tenets of capitalism" and concluded that "More Federal Reserve fixing of interest rates and credit expansion can hardly solve our problems when this has been precisely the cause of the mess in which we currently find ourselves."[8]

After the Federal Reserve orchestrated the bailout of the hedge fund Long-Term Capital Management LP, Paul Krugman argued that "deregulation" had helped to make markets "more 'liquid'" so that "aggressive speculators are able to leverage themselves", as Long-Term Capital Management had done.[9] But this explanation begged the question of *why* a company would choose to put itself at such risk; after all, it is not in a business's own self-interest to drive itself into bankruptcy.

Ron Paul offered some insights into that question in the House of Representatives. He brought up the "taxpayer-backed liability concerns raised by the involvement of an agency"—the Federal Reserve Bank of New York—"with the full faith and credit of the U.S. government" through the Federal Deposit Insurance Corporation (FDIC). The implicit promise of future intervention to bail out financial institutions created a "moral hazard" that could incentivize greater risk-taking with the knowledge that any losses would ultimately be incurred by the taxpayers. He urged the Congress to consider "the potential for systemic risk posed by any future episode that might involve the imprudent use of derivatives and excessive amounts of leverage."[10]

In June 1999, Paul Krugman wrote that "something a little strange is going on" because consumers were spending so madly rather than saving "for a rainy day." "Consumer spending traditionally lags behind the economy as a whole in boom times," he said. "This time, however, consumers are leading the charge". He raised the question of "whether America's consumption boom is really a good thing", pointing out that consumers were being "imprudent in spending so much", with personal savings having "disappeared almost completely". He reasoned that spending was so high because many people were investing in the stock market, and others were "trying to keep up with the Gateses" even though they "really can't afford it". He nevertheless argued that the high level of consumption was "good for producers" and helped to "create jobs", which had "allowed the United States economy to sail through a global financial storm unscathed, and arguably made the difference between a global wobble and a repeat of the 1930's." He remarked that "those rats racing in their cages are what have kept the wheels of commerce turning" during "America's consumer-led boom".[11]

Thus, while Ron Paul was warning of a bursting bubble and imminent recession, Krugman continued to reassure readers that the U.S. economy was in fundamentally sound condition. While Ron Paul was warning of the danger of people spending beyond their means, Paul Krugman was hailing excessive consumerism as a positive force for job creation that had helped to insulate the U.S. economy from the financial troubles other countries were facing. Additionally, Krugman's explanation for this excessive spending begged the question of *why* people would try to "keep up with the Gateses" when it meant spending beyond their means. While Krugman thus ignored the role of the Fed's inflationary monetary policy, Ron Paul had explained that when interest rates are high, it encourages savings, but when the Fed artificially lowers interest rates, the incentive is to borrow and to spend, rather than to save dollars that would have less purchasing power tomorrow than today.

In November 1999, Ron Paul again warned that, in addition to fueling borrowing and spending, inflation was showing up in the rising prices in assets, rather than consumer goods. The Fed's monetary policy was responsible for this financial bubble, he said. He further criticized that the government-sponsored enterprises (GSEs) Freddie Mac and Fannie Mae were contributing to the problem by encouraging Krugman's proverbial rat race, with their balance sheets showing a fourfold increase in new home borrowings. In addition, he warned that their securitization of mortgages might reduce risk for individual financial institutions, but increased the risk to the economy as a whole. This spelled trouble when coupled with the government's longstanding policy of bailing out

The Dot-Com Bubble

troubled institutions, which created a moral hazard and put the taxpayers on the hook for the risky business practices. Such government interventions in the market, he argued, did not bode well for the future.[12]

On January 5, 2000, Paul Krugman wrote that "investors aren't entirely rational" and so "stocks surge and plunge for no good reason". The markets had "suddenly dived" the day before, with people presumably having been "spooked" because "everyone—me included—is even more confused than usual about what stocks are really worth these days." He downplayed the stock market drop by saying that "current stock prices already have built in the expectation of economic performance that not long ago we would have considered incredible; performance that is merely terrific would be seen as a big letdown." Thus, in Krugman's view, the dip was merely a signal of a "merely terrific" rather than "incredible" economy. His forecast for the future came down to the question, "So which will it be—terrific or incredible?" Thus, in his view, there was no place for the economy to go but up, and he was oblivious to the stock market bubble and impending bust. He closed by writing optimistically, "But hey, it's still a terrific economy. Or do I mean incredible?"[13]

In February 2000, Krugman again hailed the "booming" economy and "extraordinary prosperity" the country was experiencing.[14] As the bubble neared its peak, he commented on the view that "the whole stock market, not just the Dow, is inflated by a speculative bubble". He said that he was "sympathetic but not entirely convinced" of this view. "I'm not sure that the current value of the NASDAQ is justified, but I'm not sure that it isn't."[15] Thus, on the eve of it bursting, Krugman was still not convinced of the existence of the bubble Ron Paul had already been warning about for years.

Even after the NASDAQ began to plummet, Krugman could still write that "the U.S. economy has cheerfully broken all the old limits" with "almost every fresh economic statistic" having been "a cause for celebration." He evidently believed that the economy was not facing a recession, but merely a period of lesser growth. He remained convinced that there was nowhere to go but up; there must be a "speed limit", and "growth will have to slow", but it would continue.[16]

While Krugman was predicting continued growth, Ron Paul was telling his fellow Congressmen that the coming recession could not be prevented:

[Fed as counterfeit money]

Ron Paul vs. Paul Krugman

> Business cycles are well understood. They are not a natural consequence of capitalism but instead from central bank manipulation of credit.... The next downturn, likewise, will be the fault of the Fed.... The silly notion that money can be created at will by a printing press or through computer entries is eagerly accepted by the majority as an easy road to riches, while ignoring any need for austerity, hard work, saving, and a truly free market economy.... But that's a fallacy. There is always a cost. Artificially low interest rates prompt lower savings, over-capacity expansion, malinvestment, excessive borrowing, speculation, and price increases in various segments of the economy.[17]

In October 2000, Ron Paul observed that with the ongoing financial crisis, politicians and economists were "talking about a symptom and not the cause. The cause is the Federal Reserve. The problem is that the Federal Reserve has been granted authority that is unconstitutional to go and counterfeit money, and until we recognize that and deal with that, we will continue to have financial problems."[18] He repeated, "We have already seen signs of economic troubles ahead" because the Fed had planned to continue its monetary inflation in answer to the financial crisis. "Without savings, true capital investment cannot be maintained," he said. "Creation of credit out of thin air by the Fed was the original problem, so it surely can't be the solution."[19]

In December 2000, Paul Krugman returned to his comparison of the Federal Reserve's influence on the economy as a driver operating a vehicle. "Alan Greenspan and his colleagues try to keep the economy on a steady course", he said, but "managing the economy is like trying to drive a car whose brakes have an uncertain and delayed effect on its speed."

> For more than a year the Fed has been tapping on those brakes, trying to slow an economy that it thought was growing too fast. Until a few weeks ago the higher interest rates didn't seem to be having much effect. Now there are signs that consumers are feeling cautious, a state of mind that isn't helped by the plunge in tech stocks. Meanwhile, low stock prices and high interest rates on corporate bonds are cramping business investment. So

now it seems that the Fed may have stayed on the brakes a little too long.

He mentioned the possibility of a recession, remarking, "But even if we do have a recession, so what?" A "brief recession" would not "reflect any fundamental problems in the economy."[20]

While Krugman continued to reassure his readers that the economy was fundamentally sound and allaying fears of a recession, Ron Paul continued to criticize the Fed's monetary policy, which "causes and brings about a boom period in a cycle, but it also brings about the bust because the bust, the correction, is the inevitable consequence of the boom caused by unduly inflating the money supply." He predicted that "Soon we will hear from many, we have already heard some from the financial circles as well as from politicians, to lower interest rates." This, he cautioned, "is a serious mistake."

> The only way the Federal Reserve can lower interest rates is by inflating the money supply, increasing the money supply, which is the cause of our problems. So if the cause of our problem is the inflation, increasing the money supply which causes a boom, we can hardly solve our problems by further inflating.[21]

Paul Krugman was among those who soon thereafter began calling for the Fed to lower interest rates. He wrote that the economy was "going through its roughest patch in years, with panicky analysts and self-interested politicians declaring that the sky is falling". However, he reassured, "recessions are not a serious problem for large, modern economies" because "recessionary tendencies can usually be effectively treated with cheap, over-the-counter medication: cut interest rates a couple of percentage points, provide plenty of liquidity, and call me in the morning." He assured that the "slowdown is just one of those things that happen now and then; it doesn't indicate any fundamental flaws in our economic policy, any need to do anything except cut interest rates.... We don't need to fear a recession; if it does happen, it's something that the Fed can easily cure."[22]

As for the now burst bubble, Krugman explained it by saying that "the error of the tech sector" had been "overestimating the demand for its services".[23]

But Krugman's explanation begged the question: *how* could entrepreneurs and investors across an entire sector of the economy make such a collective error in judgment? While Krugman ignored the question, Ron Paul had already provided a clear and concise answer in terms of the Austrian theory of the business cycle.

The Housing Bubble

Paul Krugman wrote in early January 2001 that the soaring NASDAQ had been "a classic bubble"—which raised the question of why he had failed to recognize it at the time. He was no longer reassuring his readers of continued slow growth. Rather, with the NASDAQ plummeting, he acknowledged the increasing possibility of a recession, although he continued to express uncertainty that it would occur.[24] Several weeks later, he praised the Fed for cutting interest rates, saying that "the Fed's move has already made a noticeable difference, stemming the rout in the NASDAQ and producing a striking recovery in the corporate bond market. Another few shots in the arm like that and talk of recession might well evaporate."[25]

While Krugman was convinced that his prescribed medicine was working to cure the economy, Ron Paul continued to characterize that same policy as poison, stating that government and Fed

> officials have repeatedly argued that we have no inflation to fear. Yet those who claim this define inflation as rising consumer and producer prices. Although inflation frequently leads to price increases we must remember that the free market definition of inflation is the increase in the supply of money and credit. Monetary inflation is seductive in that it can cause great harm without significantly affecting government price indices. The excess credit may well go into stock market and real estate speculation....[26]

Thus, as early as February 14, 2001, Ron Paul was already warning against the creation of another bubble, and identifying housing as one sector in which it might occur.

Krugman continued to downplay fears of a recession with the argument that "The Fed can easily and quickly cut interest rates as much as necessary, as long as zero is low enough."[27] In March, he expressed concern that Alan Greenspan "may be getting behind the curve on his proper job, the management of the economy." The Fed had "resisted calls for another emergency interest-rate cut", which "might turn out to be a big mistake."[28] That is to say, in Krugman's view, the Fed was not throwing enough money at the problem and needed to cut interest rates further to prevent the recession.

In March 2001, Krugman indirectly derided the argument Ron Paul had been making, and the Austrian theory of the business cycle, when he ridiculed what he called "the 'hangover theory'", which said that following a bubble, the economy must go through a recession.

> The hangover theory has a strong emotional appeal. It turns the prosaic realities of the business cycle into a morality play of sin, punishment and redemption. But it doesn't actually make any sense. During a financial bubble many bad investments get made. So what? The nation should write those investments off and move on. There are other productive investments to be made, other good uses for the economy's resources. And if people are hesitant about spending enough money to keep those resources employed, well, the central bank should just cut interest rates until spending money is an opportunity too good to refuse.

In other words, no recession was required to liquidate the debt and malinvestment from an artificial boom; the bad investments could simply be somehow written off and the Fed could cut interest rates to encourage spending elsewhere and keep the economy going strong. If there was a recession, he concluded, "the fault will lie not in ourselves, but in our central bankers, who acted too little, too late. And it will be the Federal Reserve's responsibility to get us out again."[29]

But Krugman was once again begging the question. If the Austrian theory of the business cycle was correct, and artificially low interest rates had caused those "bad investments" in the first place, how could cutting interest rates to encourage even more spending also be the solution? If this form of price fixing had allowed the malinvestment to go unidentified for so long in the first place, how could it be identified in order to write it off and move on so long as the price fixing continued rather than allowing the market to determine interest rates?

As the market continued to plunge, Krugman commented, "It goes without saying that the Fed must cut interest rates next week. And too small a cut will be almost as bad as no cut at all."[30] Shortly thereafter, he criticized the Fed for a "half-hearted" interest rate cut of half a percent "amid hopes that it would act decisively to stop the slide in America's economic growth."[31]

On May 2, 2001, Krugman again dismissed the Austrian business cycle theory, which he this time called "a sort of crime-and-punishment theory of recessions", which said "that after the economy goes through a period of speculative excess, it must then pay for that excess with a slump." Financial bubbles, which he attributed to "irrational exuberance", did not need to be followed by a recession, he repeated. "Millions of Americans have decided that low interest rates offer a good opportunity to refinance their homes or buy new ones", he argued. Rates should be "cut quickly enough to stimulate alternative investments", such as in housing. He blamed the busts that follow booms on the Federal Reserve being "too slow to cut interest rates in the face of a burst bubble". He praised Greenspan for having cut rates by the time of his writing, but called for "at least one more rate cut, please".[32]

In July 2001, Krugman wrote:

> It wasn't true when Richard Nixon said it, but it is true today: We are all Keynesians now…. When it comes to the U.S. economy, everyone … in practice views the current slowdown in terms of the intellectual framework John Maynard Keynes created 65 years ago. In particular, everyone thinks that during a slump what we need is more spending. Before Keynes, the general view was quite the opposite: economic slumps were supposed to be the invisible hand's way of punishing excesses, and the best cure was supposed to be a good dose of austerity, public and private. Only as a result of the Keynesian revolution did it become obvious to everyone—so obvious that people take it for granted—that the problem during a slump is too little spending, not too much, and

that recovery depends on persuading the public to start spending again.

Krugman commented further that "you would have to search far and wide to find anyone … who thinks that the Fed is wrong to cut interest rates in the face of a slump."[33]

Inasmuch as it applied to Austrian business cycle theory, Krugman's argument was a fallacy, for the simple fact that he continued to focus on "the problem during a slump". He continued to diagnose the disease as being the bust, rather than addressing the argument that the bust was merely the *symptom* of the disease, which was the artificial boom brought about through inflationary monetary policy. As for those who argued that cutting interest rates was the wrong "solution" to a recession, one needn't have searched too far or too wide. One could hear a voice crying in the wilderness on the floor of the House of Representatives in Washington, D.C.

Krugman appeared with Lou Dobbs on Moneyline the same day, where he repeated that the Fed needed to lower interest rates to spur investment in in "things like housing". He stated that "all of the major recessions we've had for the last 40 years have been basically caused by the Fed." Ron Paul would certainly have agreed; however, Krugman did not blame the Fed for creating artificial booms in the first place, but rather for "raising interest rates to bring inflation down", which he identified as the cause of the bust. The explanation he offered for the cause of the bubble was simply "overinvestment".[34]

By the end of July, Krugman conceded that his medicine wasn't working, but argued that this was because the dose just wasn't high enough. While short-term interest rates had been cut, long-term rates had remained "stubbornly high". This, he argued, was "just supply and demand", because bond traders were anticipating a future increase in the supply of bonds because of the shrinking budget surplus, which Krugman attributed to the Bush administration tax cut (as opposed to excessive government spending). He criticized Alan Greenspan for having endorsed the tax cut.[35]

While wishing for further interest rate cuts, Krugman dismissed any concerns about inflation, arguing that "the dollar's inevitable decline … will be a good thing for our economy" because a "weaker dollar … makes U.S. goods cheaper compared with the products of other countries" and thus boost exports. Blaming the recession in part a strong dollar, he argued that "the U.S. economy has stumbled, and the strong

The Housing Bubble

dollar is one of the reasons the Fed is having trouble pulling us back from the brink." Krugman's solution was thus again simply to run the printing presses and inflate the country's way to prosperity.[36]

On August 14, 2001, Krugman wrote that three years before, "after the collapse of Long Term Capital Management, U.S. financial markets were in crisis", but then "the Fed surprised markets by cutting rates" and "Alan Greenspan was promoted to demigod status." Krugman acknowledged that although Greenspan "has cut again and again" throughout the year, there were "few signs that a turnaround is imminent." His proposed solution was to up the dose of his medicine:

> To reflate the economy, the Fed doesn't have to restore business investment; any kind of increase in demand will do. How might demand increase? Consumers, who already have low savings and high debt, probably can't contribute much. But housing, which is highly sensitive to interest rates, could help lead a recovery.... But there has been a peculiar disconnect between Fed policy and the financial variables that affect housing and trade. Housing demand depends on long-term rather than short-term interest rates—and though the Fed has cut short rates from 6.5 to 3.75 percent since the beginning of the year, the 10-year rate is slightly higher than it was on Jan. 1.

Thus, all the Fed needed to do was to lower long-term interest rates in order to spur investment in the housing sector.[37]

On with Lou Dobbs again on August 22, 2001, Krugman reiterated his prescription, saying that he was "a little depressed" because in "[h]ousing, long-term rates haven't fallen enough to produce a boom there".[38] At the end of the month, he commented optimistically that Fed "keeps on cutting rates, hoping that it will finally accomplish something"—a tacit acknowledgment that his medicine wasn't doing the trick.[39] In September, he repeated that "the odds are still that rate cuts will eventually work."[40]

On September 6, 2001, Ron Paul warned that the monetary policy Krugman was advocating was creating a housing bubble that would inevitably require a correction. He also commented that the securitization of mortgages posed an additional risk, and that the consequences for the economy when this housing bubble burst would be even more harmful than simply allowing the recession resulting from the bursting of the dot-com bubble to occur, and would threaten the entire global economy. His prescient remarks are worth quoting at length:

> The Federal Reserve credit created during the last eight months has not stimulated economic growth in technology or the industrial sector, but a lot of it ended up in the expanding real-estate bubble, churned by the $3.2 trillion of debt maintained by the GSEs. The GSEs, made up of Fannie Mae, Freddie Mac, and the Federal Home Loan Bank, have managed to keep the housing market afloat, in contrast to the more logical slowdown in hotel and office construction. This spending through the GSEs has also served as a vehicle for consumption spending. This should be no surprise, considering the special status that GSEs enjoy, since their implied line of credit to the U.S. Treasury keeps interest rates artificially low. The Clinton administration encouraged growth in housing loans that were financed through this system.
>
> In addition, the Federal Reserve treats GSE securities with special consideration. Ever since the fall of 1999, the Fed has monetized GSE securities, just as if they were U.S. Treasury bills. This message has not been lost by foreign central banks, which took their cue from the Fed and now hold more than $130 billion of United States GSE securities. The Fed holds only $20 billion worth, but the implication is clear. Not only will the Treasury loan to the GSEs if necessary, since the line of credit is already in place, but, if necessary, Congress will surely accommodate with appropriations as well, just as it did during the Savings and Loan crisis. But the Fed has indicated to the world that the GSEs are equivalent to U.S. Treasury bills, and foreign central banks have enthusiastically accommodated, sometimes by purchasing more than $10 billion of these securities in one week alone. They are merely recycling the dollars we so generously print and spend overseas.

The Housing Bubble

[Margin note: Economists like evolutionary biologists — clever models, highly intelligent — thinking themselves wise they became fools.]

After the NASDAQ collapsed last year, the flow of funds into real estate accelerated. The GSEs accommodated, by borrowing without restraint to subsidize new mortgages, record sales and refinancing. It's no wonder the price of houses are rising to record levels. Refinancing especially helped the consumers to continue spending even in a slowing economy. It isn't surprising for high credit-card debt to be frequently rolled into second mortgages, since interest on mortgage debt has the additional advantage of being tax-deductible. When financial conditions warrant it, leaving financial instruments (such as paper assets), and looking for hard assets (such as houses), is commonplace and is not a new phenomenon. Instead of the newly inflated money being directed toward the stock market, it now finds its way into the rapidly expanding real-estate bubble. This, too, will burst as all bubbles do.

The Fed, the Congress, or even foreign investors can't prevent the collapse of this bubble, any more than the incestuous Japanese banks were able to keep the Japanese "miracle" of the 1980s going forever. Concerned Federal Reserve economists are struggling to understand how the wealth effect of the stock market and real estate bubble affect economic activity and consumer spending. It should be no mystery, but it would be too much to expect the Fed to look to itself and its monetary policy for an explanation and assume responsibility for engineering the entire financial mess we're in.

A major problem still remains. ==Ultimately, the market determines all value including all currencies.== With the current direction of the dollar certainly downward, the day of reckoning is fast approaching. A weak dollar will prompt dumping of GSE securities before treasuries, despite the Treasury's and the Fed's attempt to equate them with government securities. This will threaten the whole GSE system of finance, because the challenge to the dollar and the GSEs will hit just when the housing market turns down and defaults rise. Also a major accident can occur in the derivatives markets where

21

Fannie Mae and Freddie Mac are deeply involved in hedging their interest-rate bets. Rising interest rates that are inherent with a weak currency will worsen the crisis. The weakening dollar will usher in an age of challenge to the whole worldwide financial system....

Federal Reserve officials and other government leaders purposely continue to mislead the people by spouting the nonsense that there is no evidence of inflation, as measured by government-rigged price indices. Even though significant price increases need not exist for monetary inflation to place a hardship on the economy, stock prices, housing prices, costs of medical care and education, and the cost of government have all been rising at very rapid rates.... The deception regarding price increases is supposed to reassure us and may do so for a while. The Fed never admits it, and the Congress disregards it out of ignorance, but the serious harm done by artificially low interest rates—leading to malinvestment, overcapacity, excessive debt and speculation causes the distortions that always guarantee the next recession. Serious problems lie ahead. If the Fed continues with the same monetary policy of perpetual inflation, and the Congress responds with more spending and regulations, real solutions will be indefinitely delayed.[41]

Three days after the terrorist attacks of September 11, 2001, Paul Krugman wrote that "Ghastly as it may seem to say this, the terror attack—like the original day of infamy, which brought an end to the Great Depression—could even do some economic good." He argued, "If people rush out to buy bottled water and canned goods, that will actually boost the economy", and "rebuilding will generate at least some increase in business spending."[42] Krugman thus repeated the old "broken window" fallacy identified by Frederic Bastiat a century-and-a-half before.[43]

He repeated the fallacy again in an article in the *New York Times Magazine* on September 30, 2001, in which he also repeated that the "first line of defense against an economic slump" was "to cut interest rates", which would "persuade businesses and consumers to borrow and spend,

The Housing Bubble

which creates new jobs, which encourages people to spend even more, and so on." Again blaming the stock bubble on "irrational exuberance", he remarked that "a few lonely voices" had warned of a bubble.

> But conventional wisdom said that this was nonsense, that our mature financial markets would never get that out of touch with reality. When stock prices reached multiples of earnings that were way above historical norms, some warned that it was indeed a Japanese-style bubble. But conventional wisdom said that this was nonsense, that the New Economy justified those higher multiples. When our bubble finally burst, some warned that we might have a Japanese-style recession. But conventional wisdom said that this was nonsense, that the economy was more resilient than that. And when the slowdown came, some warned that we might find it as hard as the Japanese did to turn it around. But conventional wisdom said that this was nonsense, that the great Greenspan would soon set things right.

Notice that when Krugman here spoke of "conventional wisdom", he was in fact referring to the "wisdom" he himself had embraced (this is, as will be seen further, a common literary device he employs, apparently in an attempt to avoid self-criticism and any admission that he had been wrong).

"Housing was doing better, thanks to low interest rates," he continued, "but some analysts were warning about a housing bubble", and the interest rate cuts hadn't turned the economy around. Krugman's worry was that the Fed might zero interest rates and the economy would continue to decline; but the Fed could still do a lot if it was "willing to abandon conventional notions of prudence", such as by purchasing long-term government debt in addition to short-term securities. This was a "radical" idea "branded as irresponsible" when it "first came out", but had "since become respectable, almost mainstream." Krugman's "nightmare" scenario included his fear that "the housing bubble bursts and we have another slump".[44] He thus cannot possibly claim to have been unaware of the possible, even likely, danger that cutting long-term interest rates—an idea previously considered "radical" and "irresponsible"—would create a housing bubble that would simply result

23

in yet another recession. It was nevertheless the policy course he resolutely advocated.

On October 7, 2001, Krugman wrote that "economic policy should encourage other spending to offset the temporary slump in business investment. Low interest rates, which promote spending on housing and other durable goods, are the main answer."[45]

Ron Paul continued to warn against Krugman's solution to the problem:

> We are now witnessing the early stages of the demise of a world-wide financial system built on the fiction that wealth can come out of a printing press or a computer at our central banks…. More bailouts from the IMF and the U.S. dollar may temper the crisis for a short time, but ultimately it will only hurt the dollar and U.S. taxpayers…. Printing money is not an answer. Yet that is all that is offered. The clamor for low interest rates by all those who benefit from fiat money has prompted the Fed to create new money out of thin air like never before…. This policy reflects the central bank's complete ignorance as to the cause of the problem—credit creation and manipulation of interest rates…. Nothing can correct the problems we face if we do not give up on the foolishness of fiat. Mr. Speaker, a dollar crisis is quickly approaching. We should prepare ourselves.[46]

Krugman wrote at the end of 2001 that "the Fed has now cut interest rates 11 times this year, and has yet to see any results". Although it hadn't cured the patient as he had hoped, Krugman believed his medicine was nevertheless working and all that was needed was a stronger dose. He argued that long-term interest rates were being kept too high, which helped to ensure that the Fed would not be able to "conjure up another dramatic boom".[47] While the economy was in the very recession Krugman had earlier dismissed, he remained optimistic, celebrating the "good news" that "it didn't fall off a cliff." He praised "the Fed's dramatic interest rate cuts", which had "helped keep housing strong".[48]

In February 2002, Paul Krugman touted the idea that even useless spending was good for the economy. "The only clear force for recovery I see", he wrote, "is the administration's military splurge. After all, even useless weapons spending does create jobs, at least for a while." In that case, why not simply have the government hire a bunch of people to dig a bunch of holes, and another group of people to fill them back in again? After all, that, too, would "create jobs", and no blood would have to be shed to get the job done.[49]

In the wake of the Enron scandal, many people responded by calling for more regulation. Ron Paul, however, argued that "more red tape" would not solve anything. "The real problem with SEC rules is that they give investors a false sense of security, a sense that the government is protecting them from dangerous investments." The solution was not to place more trust in the government to look out for investors. "If anything," he said, "the Enron failure should teach us to place less trust in the SEC."

He also commented on how the Fed had created an "easy credit environment" that "made it possible for Enron to secure hundreds of millions in uncollateralized loans, loans that now cannot be repaid." Loans from the Export-Import Bank were effectively "taxpayer subsidies to large, politically-powerful bankruptcies such as Enron". Instead of blaming capitalism, he said, "we should focus on repealing those monetary and fiscal policies that distort the market and allow the politically powerful to enrich themselves at the expense of the American taxpayer."[50]

On February 7, 2002, he repeated his warning of another bubble resulting from Fed monetary policy:

> It is precisely too much government, and especially manipulation of credit by the Federal Reserve, that precipitated the economic downturn in the first place. Increasing that which caused the recession can't possibly, at the same time, be the solution…. Every recession in the last 30 years, since the dollar became a purely fiat currency, has ended after a significant correction and resumption of all the bad policies that caused the recession in the first place. Each rebound required more spending, debt and easy credit than the previous recovery did. And with each cycle, the government got bigger and more intrusive….
>
> Because of our unique position as the economic powerhouse of the world, we're able to borrow more

> than anyone else. Foreigners loan us exorbitant sums, as our current account deficit soars out of sight. The U.S. now has a foreign debt of over $2 trillion. Perceptions and illusions and easy credit allow our consumers to spend, even in recessions, by rolling up even more debt in a time when market forces are saying that borrowing should decrease and the debt burden lessen.... If we do not change our ways, the financial bubble will just go back to inflating again.[51]

He further criticized the government policy of encouraging homeownership, stating that "federal housing subsidies distort the housing market by taking capital that could be better used elsewhere, and applying it to housing at the direction of politicians and bureaucrats."[52] He also criticized the FDIC for creating a moral hazard, since premiums paid by financial institutions were the principle source of money for the deposit insurance fund, which was then used to bail out banks unable to meet their commitments to depositors.

> Thus, the deposit insurance system transfers liability for poor management decisions from those who made the decisions to their competitors. This system punishes those financial institutions which follow sound practices, as they are forced to absorb the losses of their competitors. This also compounds the moral hazard problem created whenever government socializes business losses. In the event of a severe banking crisis, Congress likely will transfer funds from general revenues into the Deposit Insurance Fund, which could make all taxpayers liable for the mistakes of a few.[53]

While Ron Paul continued to warn that government intervention in the market was creating a housing bubble that would lead to a financial crisis and bailouts that would fall on the backs of taxpayers, Paul Krugman acclaimed how "residential investment kept rising through the recession, thanks to the Fed's interest rate cuts." While still confident in his prescription, however, he was no longer proclaiming that the Fed should just cut interest rates and call him in the morning. "It's hard to see a dramatic further increase; if anything, housing may be in a mild bubble. So what will lead us into a full-fledged recovery? Beats me."[54]

On July 9, 2002, Ron Paul again warned about the housing bubble that Paul Krugman believed could possibly lead to "a full-fledged recovery":

> Nixon was right—once—when he declared "We're all Keynesians now." All of Washington is in sync in declaring that too much capitalism has brought us to where we are today. The only decision now before the central planners in Washington is whose special interests will continue to benefit from the coming pretense at reform....
>
> But what is not discussed is the actual cause and perpetration of the excesses now unraveling at a frantic pace.... Easy credit became the holy grail of monetary policy, especially under Alan Greenspan, "the ultimate Maestro." ... Monetary inflation continues at a rate never seen before in a frantic effort to prop up stock prices and continue the housing bubble, while avoiding the consequences that inevitably come from easy credit....
>
> To condemn free-market capitalism because of anything going on today makes no sense. There is no evidence that capitalism exists today. We are deeply involved in an interventionist-planned economy that allows major benefits to accrue to the politically connected of both political spectrums. One may condemn the fraud and the current system, but it must be called by its proper names—Keynesian inflationism, interventionism, and corporatism.[55]

On July 15, 2002, Ron Paul again warned that government interference in the market would result in a crash in the housing market. He introduced legislation to repeal "special privileges for housing-related government sponsored enterprises (GSEs)" such as Fannie Mae and Freddie Mac, which had "received $13.6 billion worth of indirect federal subsidies in fiscal year 2000 alone." He explained further:

> One of the major government privileges granted these GSEs is a line of credit to the United States Treasury.

According to some estimates, the line of credit may be worth over $2 billion. This explicit promise by the Treasury to bail out these GSEs in times of economic difficulty helps them attract investors who are willing to settle for lower yields than they would demand in the absence of the subsidy. Thus, the line of credit distorts the allocation of capital. More importantly, the line of credit is a promise on behalf of the government to engage in a massive unconstitutional and immoral income transfer from working Americans to holders of GSE debt....

Ironically, by transferring the risk of a widespread mortgage default, the government increases the likelihood of a painful crash in the housing market. This is because the special privileges of Fannie, Freddie, and HLBB [National Home Loan Bank Board] have distorted the housing market by allowing them to attract capital they could not attract under pure market conditions. As a result, capital is diverted from its most productive use into housing. This reduces the efficacy of the entire market and thus reduces the standard of living of all Americans.

However, despite the long-term damage to the economy inflicted by the government's interference in the housing market, the government's policies of diverting capital to other uses creates a short-term boom in housing. Like all artificially-created bubbles, the boom in housing prices cannot last forever. When housing prices fall, homeowners will experience difficulty as their equity is wiped out. Furthermore, the holders of the mortgage debt will also have a loss. These losses will be greater than they would have otherwise been had government policy not actively encouraged over-investment in housing.

Perhaps the Federal Reserve can stave off the day of reckoning by purchasing GSE debt and pumping liquidity into the housing market, but this cannot hold off the

The Housing Bubble

inevitable drop in the housing market forever. In fact, postponing the necessary but painful market corrections will only deepen the inevitable fall....

Mr. Speaker, it is time for Congress to act to remove taxpayer support from the housing GSEs before the bubble bursts and taxpayers are once again forced to bail out investors misled by foolish government interference in the market.[56]

Paul Krugman stuck to his own prescription of throwing more money at the problem. "Given the definitely iffy economic outlook," he wrote in his column, "shouldn't Mr. Greenspan be thinking seriously about another interest rate cut?"[57]

On August 2, 2002, Krugman wrote an article in which he said that what the Fed needed to do in order to prevent a recession was to create a housing bubble. His statement, quoted in its full context, was as follows:

A few months ago the vast majority of business economists mocked concerns about a "double dip," a second leg to the downturn. But there were a few dogged iconoclasts out there, most notably Stephen Roach at Morgan Stanley. As I've repeatedly said in this column, the arguments of the double-dippers made a lot of sense. And their story now looks more plausible than ever.

The basic point is that the recession of 2001 wasn't a typical postwar slump, brought on when an inflation-fighting Fed raises rates and easily ended by a snapback in housing and consumer spending when the Fed brings rates back down again. This was a prewar-style recession, a morning after brought on by irrational exuberance. To fight this recession the Fed needs more than a snapback; it needs soaring household spending to offset moribund business investment. And to do that, as Paul McCulley of PIMCO put it, Alan Greenspan needs to create a housing bubble to replace the NASDAQ bubble.

Judging by Mr. Greenspan's remarkably cheerful recent testimony, he still thinks he can pull that off. But the Fed chairman's crystal ball has been cloudy lately; remember how he urged Congress to cut taxes to head off the risk of excessive budget surpluses? And a sober look at recent data is not encouraging.

Curiously, he commented that Alan Greenspan needed a recovery "to avoid awkward questions about his own role in creating the stock market bubble", but didn't elaborate on what that role *was*. He closed by saying, "But wishful thinking aside, I just don't understand the grounds for optimism. Who, exactly, is about to start spending a lot more?"[58]

It is important to be clear on what Krugman was saying here. His earlier record on the housing bubble is unambiguous. He had repeatedly advocated that the Fed should lower interest rates for the explicit purpose of creating a boom in housing as a route to economic recovery. Here, he was implicitly acknowledging that the numerous interest rate cuts that had already been made had not solved the problem. The reason he offered was that people were still not spending enough, and his argument had been that the Fed should cut interest rates even further. He attributed the view that the Fed "needs to create a housing bubble" to Paul McCulley, but there can be no mistake, reading his remark in context, that Krugman was in agreement. This is evident in his prefacing the remark by saying that people warning of a double-dip recession "made a lot of sense", by his own (not McCulley's) comment that to "fight the recession" the Fed "needs" to do so, and by his expressed pessimism that the Fed could "pull that off".

Later that month, Krugman said that the "economic funk" was "not over". He wrote that there was "no mystery about the cause of our funk". The problem in his view was that "the bubble years left us with too much capacity, too much debt and a backlog of business scandal." The question remained: *why* had such malinvestment occurred? What Krugman identified as the disease, Ron Paul had identified as the symptoms. Furthermore, if "too much debt" was admittedly part of the *problem*, how, then, could Krugman possibly rationalize advocating a Fed policy of encouraging even *more* spending and *more* debt as the *solution*?

Krugman further wrote that he was "getting worried" that the U.S. might "have a real estate bubble". "More and more people are using the B-word about the housing market", and there were suggestions that "people are now buying houses for speculation rather than merely for shelter." So what was Krugman's answer to the possibility of a housing bubble? To cut interest rates further and "throw money at the economy", of course!

> If we do have a housing bubble, and it bursts, we'll be looking a lot too [*sic*] Japanese for comfort. A recent Federal Reserve analysis of Japan's experience declares that the key mistake Japan made in the early 1990's was "not that policy makers did not predict the oncoming deflationary slump—after all, neither did most forecasters—but that they did not take out sufficient insurance against downside risks through a precautionary further loosening of monetary policy." That's Fedspeak for "if you think deflation is even a possibility, throw money at the economy now and don't worry about overdoing it." And yet the Fed chose not to cut rates on Tuesday. Why?[59]

On September 10, 2002, Ron Paul introduced "legislation to restore financial stability to America's economy by abolishing the Federal Reserve". He explained:

> Since the creation of the Federal Reserve, middle and working-class Americans have been victimized by a boom-and-bust monetary policy. In addition, most Americans have suffered a steadily eroding purchasing power because of the Federal Reserve's inflationary policies. This represents a real, if hidden, tax imposed on the American people. From the Great Depression, to the stagflation of the seventies, to the burst of the dot-com bubble last year, every economic downturn suffered by the country over the last 80 years can be traced to Federal Reserve policy. The Fed has followed a consistent policy of flooding the economy with easy money, leading to a misallocation of resources and an artificial "boom" followed by a recession or depression when the Fed-created bubble bursts.[60]

In October 2002, Paul Krugman again acknowledged that the Fed's low-interest rates weren't working out quite the way he had hoped: "Industrial production is falling and layoffs are rising.... [I]t looks as if the economy is stalling.... And the job situation is increasingly dismal.... [I]n terms of job losses and long-term unemployment, the current slowdown is already a match for the nasty recession of the early 1990's." There was "concern that interest rate cuts by the Fed might not be enough to turn the economy around".[61] He nevertheless continued to praise the Fed for having "cut rates early and often", lauding that "those 11 interest rate cuts in 2001 fueled a boom both in housing purchases and in mortgage refinancing, both of which helped keep the economy from experiencing a much more severe recession."[62]

On October 4, 2002, Krugman wrote that the U.S. was now in a "classic overinvestment slump", and "such slumps have always been hard to fight simply by cutting interest rates." The problem, in his view, was that "the Fed hasn't done enough" and it "should cut rates further—it may not be enough, but it will help. What else should we do?" His answer was to have a "sensible plan for fiscal stimulus" that "encourages spending"! He concluded, "This isn't rocket science. It's straightforward textbook economics, applied to our actual situation."[63]

If it wasn't "rocket science", why was he now saying such recessions "have always been hard to fight simply but cutting interest rates", when he had previously dismissed concerns of a recession with comments such as: "a global slump is quite an easy thing to prevent" (August 30, 1998); "But even if we do have a recession, so what?" (December 3, 2000); "cut interest rates a couple of percentage points, provide plenty of liquidity, and call me in the morning"; "We don't need to fear a recession; if it does happen, it's something that the Fed can easily cure" (December 27, 2000); and "Another few shots in the arm like that and talk of recession might well evaporate" (January 17, 2001)? If it was so "straightforward", why had his prescription not been the cure he had said it would be? How could he boast that it wasn't "rocket science" when he had been proven so wrong?

At the end of 2002, Krugman summarized:

> Here's the story so far: In 2000 the bubble finally burst. As investors and businesses rediscovered the law of gravity, business investment plunged, and the economy slumped. Then the situation stabilized, more or less. Repeated interest rate cuts encouraged families to buy new houses and refinance their mortgages, putting cash in their pockets; yes, the tax cut also made a marginal contribution. Strong housing demand and consumer

The Housing Bubble

spending partly offset the lack of business investment. And so the economy began growing again. But it has been a jobless, joyless recovery.

So much had the Fed cut that it "has almost run out of room to cut interest rates." It could still cut long-term rates, but "it will be reluctant to try exotic, untested policies unless the economy is clearly facing deflation." The moral of his story was, "this doesn't look like a happy new year."[64]

In May of 2003, Krugman again observed that while the Fed had "cut rates early and often", it "has almost run out of room to cut" and still "the economy remains weak."[65] Even though it had followed his prescription, Krugman criticized the Fed, saying, "I used to be a great admirer of Mr. Greenspan. But something has gone very wrong with the maestro." Greenspan's "optimism is entirely based on models predicting that tax cuts and low interest rates will get the economy moving", but "that's what the models said last year, too". He aimed his sights at the tax cuts as the main failure, commenting, "Maybe tax cuts mainly for the affluent aren't as effective as the models say." The alternative conclusion that maybe the Fed's interest rate cuts hadn't been as effective as Krugman had said they would be was something he was clearly not willing to contemplate.

Could it be that what the economy needed following the bursting of the dot-com bubble was not more attempts to create artificial growth, but a market correction? Could it be that what is needed following an artificially-created boom is to allow the debt and malinvestment to be liquidated as speedily and efficiently as possible, and that by attempting to avoid a short recession by disallowing that correction, it merely prolongs the agony and sets the stage for the next artificial boom and subsequent, even more catastrophic bust? Could it be that encouraging borrowing and spending in the wake of a bubble prevents any kind of sustainable growth from occurring? Could it be that real economic growth comes from savings and capital investment, rather than from encouraging even more debt? Such possibilities were evidently beyond Krugman's willingness to comprehend.

He continued, lauding the interest rate cuts for creating a housing boom and criticizing Greenspan further for not cutting interest rates even further:

Meanwhile, the boost from low interest rates seems to be evaporating. Mortgage rates did indeed fall briefly to historic lows, extending the home-buying and refinancing boom that has helped keep the economy's head above water. Since mid-June, however, rates have been climbing rapidly. This week rates on 30-year mortgages hit their highest level since January. And Mr. Greenspan bears some of the responsibility. Until June, Fed officials had helped push down interest rates precisely by not being too optimistic—by indicating that they took concerns about deflation seriously, that they were not taking recovery for granted. Then they surprised markets with a small cut in the federal funds rate [the rate at which banks lend to each other], a move that seemed to suggest that they were taking recovery for granted, after all.[66]

In August 2003, Krugman said that the state of the economy fit neither the definition of a recession nor of a recovery, and he declared, "There's nothing particularly mysterious about our situation." The previous year, we may recall, he had said it "isn't rocket science" and all that needed to be done was to encourage spending. Now, he acknowledged that people were spending, but that the reported economic "growth" hadn't translated into relief for long-term unemployment. This meant that "while the growth and new claims numbers were good news, they didn't tell us that the economy is improving. All they said is that things are getting worse more slowly." He commented that "Consumers are spending; that's good. But rising interest rates seem to have ended the refinancing boom that put cash in consumers' pockets; that's bad."[67] The corollary was that what the economy needed was for the Fed to slash interest rates again in order to encourage homeowners to take out a second mortgage to pay off their first. If interest rate cuts hadn't led to recovery, it was just that they hadn't been cut enough. If consumer spending hadn't led to recovery, it was just that they hadn't borrowed and spent enough—they just hadn't indebted themselves enough to create economic growth.

Ron Paul continued to warn against attempting to spur "growth" by interfering in the market in this way, saying on September 5, 2003:

> Artificially low interest rates deceive investors into believing that rates are low because savings are high and

The Housing Bubble

represent funds not spent on consumption. When the Fed creates bank deposits out of thin air making loans available at below-market rates, malinvestment and overcapacity results, setting the stage for the next recession or depression. The easy credit policy is welcomed by many: stock market investors, home builders, home buyers, congressional spendthrifts, bankers, and many other consumers who enjoy borrowing at low rates and not worrying about repayment. However, perpetual good times cannot come from a printing press or easy credit created by a Federal Reserve computer. The piper will demand payment, and the downturn in the business cycle will see to it…. Lowering interest rates at times, especially early in the stages of monetary debasement, will produce the desired effects and stimulate another boom-bust cycle.[68]

In October, Krugman commented on the "impressive estimated 7.2 percent growth rate for the third quarter of 2003." He warned that people should not get their hopes up because "we've had our hopes dashed in the past" and there were "still some reasons to wonder whether the economy has really turned the corner". Among them was the fact that "the bulk of last quarter's growth came from a huge surge in consumer spending, with a further boost from housing", which "can't go on" because "in the long run, consumer spending can't outpace the growth in consumer income." It was plausible, he said, that "much of last quarter's consumer splurge was 'borrowed' from the future: consumers took advantage of low-interest financing, cash from home refinancing and tax rebate checks to accelerate purchases they would otherwise have made later." Thus, Krugman implicitly acknowledged that long-term growth had to come from savings, and not borrowing and spending encouraged by low interest rates—and yet there was no hint that this might lead him to reconsider his argument in favor of keeping rates artificially low in order to encourage borrowing and spending, specifically in the housing sector![69]

Throughout 2004, Paul Krugman wrote relatively little about monetary policy, focusing largely upon job numbers and criticizing the Bush administration's tax cut. Ron Paul continued to warn about the housing bubble, telling the House Financial Services Committee in February that the billions in subsidies to the GSEs would "distort the

35

market, create a short-term boom in housing, and endanger the economy by allowing GSEs to attract capital they could not attract under pure market conditions." Repeating that the housing bubble "cannot last forever", he predicted that mortgage debt holders would ultimately suffer financial losses and that the government's solution would be more bailouts. "A taxpayer bailout of the GSEs would dwarf the savings-and-loan bailout of the early nineties and could run up the national debt to unmanageable levels," he warned. He concluded that

> It is long past time for Congress to examine seriously the need to reform the fiat currency system. The committee also should examine how Federal Reserve policies encourage excessive public and private sector debt, and the threat that debt poses to the long-term health of the American economy.[70]

In July 2004, Ron Paul warned against excessive government spending, which had to be paid for either through taxation, borrowing, or debt monetization. "All government spending represents a tax", he explained. "The inflation tax, while largely ignored, hurts middle-class and low-income Americans the most." It was unfortunate that "no one in Washington" cared about the subject of the Federal Reserve, which was "solely responsible for inflation by creating money out of thin air. It does so either to monetize federal debt, or in the process of economic planning through interest rate manipulation." This was "destructive" to the economy and "directly responsible" for the country's "economic downturns" through "artificially low interest rates that serve the interests of big borrowers, speculators, and banks. This unfairly steals income from frugal retirees who chose to save and place their funds in interest bearing instruments like CDs."

Furthermore, the Fed acted "with essentially no Congressional oversight or understanding" and through inflation effectively imposed a tax on the American people "without legislative authority." He observed that in the past year, the Fed had expanded the M3 money supply by $700 billion, and in the first half of 2004 alone by $428 billion, a rate of increase of 10.5%. "In the last seven years the money supply has increased 80%, as M3 has soared 4.1 trillion dollars." This process disproportionately harmed the middle class, with inflation acting as a tax that transferred wealth "from the middle class to the rich". Running the printing presses to pay for "profligate government spending," he warned, "can never make a nation wealthier. But it certainly can make it poorer.[71]

His warnings went unheeded, and with the national debt having reached its limit of $7.38 trillion and as the Congress was planning to raise the ceiling by $800 billion, on November 18, 2004, Ron Paul said that

> Congress has become like the drunk who promises to sober up tomorrow, if only he can keep drinking today. Does anyone really believe this will be the last time, that Congress will tighten its belt if we just grant it one last loan? What a joke! There is only one approach to dealing with an incorrigible spendthrift: cut him off.

When the Congress spends, he repeated, the government must either "raise taxes, print more dollars, or borrow money." The increasing national debt, he said, sent the signal to investors that the government was "not serious about reining in spending" and "increases the risks that investors will be reluctant to buy government debt instruments." And if investors stopped buying government debt, he warned, "The effects on the American economy could be devastating."[72]

In April 2005, Paul Krugman wrote that the U.S. was experiencing a "mild case of stagflation: inflation is leading the Fed to tap on the brakes [i.e. raise interest rates], even though this doesn't look or feel like a full-employment economy."[73] That posed a paradox for assessing the situation through the lens of Keynesian theory, although he didn't explicitly acknowledge it.

In May, he wrote about "a return to NASDAQ-style speculative mania, this time in the housing market." But rather than discussing the Fed, Krugman talked about how China had "acted as an enabler" by buying up U.S. government debt, "insulating the U.S. economy from the effects of huge budget deficits" and keeping

> U.S. interest rates low despite the enormous government borrowing required to cover the budget deficit. Low interest rates, in turn, have been crucial to America's housing boom. And soaring house prices don't just create construction jobs; they also support consumer spending because many homeowners have converted rising house values into cash by refinancing their mortgages.

The only problem Krugman saw with this was that "if and when China changes its currency policy, and those cheap loans are no longer available", then

> U.S. interest rates will rise; the housing bubble will probably burst; construction employment and consumer spending will both fall; falling home prices may lead to a wave of bankruptcies. And we'll suddenly wonder why anyone thought financing the budget deficit was easy. In other words, we've developed an addiction to Chinese dollar purchases, and will suffer painful withdrawal symptoms when they come to an end…. And the housing bubble will eventually burst whatever we do.[74]

Krugman was clearly now cognizant of the fact that there *was* a housing bubble, and explicitly acknowledged the crucial role of low interest rates in creating it. But while rightly criticizing the growing deficit and the government's dependency on China to purchase its debt, the Fed's own role in keeping interest rates artificially low was curiously spared any scrutiny in his analysis. It should also be recognized that he wasn't suggesting that there was a problem with the housing bubble itself, but rather that the problem would be a future rise in interest rates that would cause it to burst.

As the housing bubble expanded, Krugman seemed to distance himself from his earlier position of having explicitly advocated low interest rates to create a housing boom. In his May 27, 2005 column, Krugman wrote that Paul McCulley had "predicted that the Federal Reserve would simply replace one bubble with another". Yet in his 2002 column, he hadn't characterized this as merely a *prediction*, but as a *prescription*. He also now declined to inform his readers that it had been a prescription he had agreed with.

"As Mr. McCulley predicted," Krugman continued, "interest rate cuts led to soaring home prices, which led in turn not just to a construction boom but to high consumer spending, because homeowners used mortgage refinancing to go deeper into debt. All of this created jobs to make up for those lost when the stock bubble burst." Having thus acknowledged the role of low interest rates in creating the housing bubble, Krugman continued: "Now the question is what can replace the housing bubble. Nobody thought the economy could rely forever on home buying and refinancing. But the hope was that by the

The Housing Bubble

time the housing boom petered out, it would no longer be needed." Of course, "the hope" he attributed to nobody in particular was also evidently his own.

He added that "the economy would still be in big trouble if it [the housing bubble] came to an end", and would be "right back into recession." He nevertheless maintained that creating the housing bubble in the first place was the right thing to do, because "the job losses would have been much worse if the stock bubble hadn't been quickly replaced with a housing bubble". He asked, "So what happens if the housing bubble bursts? It will be the same thing all over again, unless the Fed can find something to take its place." He commented on the view that "the Fed's apparent success after 2001 was an illusion, that it simply piled up trouble for the future". This view, he hoped, was "wrong". He concluded: "But the Fed does seem to be running out of bubbles."[75]

Once again, there can be no mistake that Krugman was advocating that the Fed should create another bubble to prevent an anticipated recession from a housing bubble that was going to burst, just as he had called for the housing bubble in the first place to prevent the bust from the dot-com bubble. This is evident in the fact that his expressed concern was that the Fed might not be able to do so! On one hand, Krugman was correctly warning that the housing bubble would burst, but on the other, he was offering a "solution" that was the same as the one that had created the problem in the first place. A useful analogy is the doctor who prescribes a medication in order for the patient to treat the symptoms the patient is suffering from. But when the patient suffers some adverse side effect from the medication, the doctor's solution is to prescribe yet another medication in order to treat the symptoms from the first, and so on. The doctor is focused on treating the symptoms the patient is suffering rather than seeking to eliminate the *cause* of those symptoms.

Again in July he repeated that "if the Chinese stopped buying all those U.S. bonds, interest rates would rise", which "would be bad news for housing—maybe very bad news, if the interest rate rise burst [*sic*] the bubble."[76] Again, the problem in his view was not that low interest rates had created a housing bubble in the first place, but that a rise in interest rates would cause it to burst. Once again, he chose not to mention the role of the Fed in creating the housing bubble.

In August 2005, Krugman again warned that people should be worried about the housing bubble bursting, but said nothing about how he had himself called for low interest rates to spur investment in the housing sector in the first place.[77] In another column, he praised that the "housing boom has created jobs" and that the economy was being "driven by real estate". Asking "What's wrong with that?" his answer was: "When that bubble begins to deflate, so will housing-related employment." Still remaining silent about the role of the Fed in creating the bubble, he remarked, "Americans make a living selling each other houses, paid for with money borrowed from the Chinese. Somehow, that doesn't seem like a sustainable lifestyle."[78] Yet, somehow, the idea of simply having the Fed print up the money to keep interest rates artificially low *did*?

In another piece, he rightly criticized Greenspan for having encouraged borrowers to take on adjustable-rate rather than fixed-rate mortgages, and for denying that there was a housing bubble, but said nothing about the role of the Fed's monetary policy in having created it. He also said that when the bubble burst and jobs were lost as a result, they wouldn't be replaced "until and unless something else, like a plunge in the value of the dollar, makes U.S. goods more competitive on world markets, leading to higher exports and lower imports."[79] Thus, once again, his implied solution to the collapse of the housing bubble he saw coming was to simply respond by running the printing presses! The very thing that he had already acknowledged was the underlying cause of the bubble was the same thing he offered again as the solution to its inevitable collapse.

In an October 2005 column, Krugman praised Bush's choice for the new Fed Chairman, Ben Bernanke (who, he disclosed, "was chairman of the Princeton economics department before moving to Washington, and he made the job offer that brought me to Princeton"). He criticized Bernanke for, like Greenspan, denying that there was a housing bubble, but once again attributed economic growth on the "unsustainable trends" of the "a huge surge in house prices and a vast inflow of funds from Asia", without any mention of the Fed's role. He closed by expressing confidence in Bernanke that, when the bubble burst, he would show the "resolve" to "start cutting interest rates".[80]

Ron Paul continued to warn that the taxpayers would be made to suffer the consequences when the housing bubble burst. The government line of credit to the GSEs and the unique privilege deriving from statutory authority from the Treasury to have their debt monetized by the Fed were contrary to the principles of a free market and endangered taxpayers. The implicit promise of a government bailout led investors to consider the GSEs a good investment without seeking assurances that they were following good management and accounting practices. In October 2005, he proposed cutting off the line of credit to institutions like Freddie Mac and Fannie Mae, saying, "I hope my colleagues join me in protecting taxpayers from having to bail out Fannie Mae and Freddie Mac when the housing bubble bursts." Rejecting the arguments being offered that more government regulation was needed, he stated, "Instead of expanding unconstitutional and market-distorting government bureaucracies, Congress should act to remove taxpayer support from the housing GSEs before the bubble bursts and taxpayers are once again forced to bail out investors who were misled by foolish government interference in the market."[81]

Unfortunately, Ron Paul's warnings went unheeded, and his predictions came to pass.

Crisis and Response

In January 2006, Krugman wrote that "In spite of record home prices, housing in most of America remains surprisingly affordable, thanks to low interest rates." But housing prices in some areas had "risen so much that housing has become much less affordable", and "with interest rates already low by historical standards, restoring affordability will require a big fall in housing prices. So here's the bottom line: yes, northern Virginia, there is a housing bubble."[82] Thus, in Krugman's view, the problem was not that artificially low interest rates had created a housing bubble, but rather that rates couldn't get much lower in order to continue to expand it!

In February, he wrote that "Sooner or later the trade deficit will have to come down, the housing boom will have to end, and both American consumers and the U.S. government will have to start living within their means". Yet there remained a complete disconnect from this cautionary remark and his perpetual policy recommendation that the Fed should keep interest rates low to encourage borrowing and spending and investment in housing.[83]

The consequences of the Fed's inflationary monetary policy went beyond the realm of economics. On February 15, 2006, Ron Paul spoke about the relationship between the Federal Reserve, inflation, and U.S. foreign policy. Printing paper money was "nothing short of counterfeiting", he said. In addition, the U.S. had the unique role of being the issuer of the world's reserve currency, and used its "military might to guarantee control over the system." The U.S. accrued economic benefits of this system in the short term, but in "the long run", it posed "a threat to the country". It allowed Americans to consume more than they produced, in the short term, but it had made the country dependent on China to buy its debt. American manufacturing jobs were meanwhile being offshored, and the trade deficit was not sustainable.

"It sounds like a great deal for everyone," he cautioned, "except the time will come when our dollars—due to their depreciation—will be received less enthusiastically or even be rejected by foreign countries. That could create a whole new ballgame and force us to pay a price for living beyond our means and our production." The current system, he said, "can't last." The stock bubble had burst, and the housing bubble was facing a similar fate. The price of gold was rising, federal spending was "out of sight with zero political will to rein it in", the trade deficit was "over $728 billion", and the U.S. was in a "$2 trillion war". "The only restraining force", he warned, "will be the world's rejection of the dollar."

He explained further that the dollar's role as the currency in which oil was traded on the world markets "has to be maintained" for the system to work, but it had already been challenged. "In November 2000, Saddam Hussein demanded euros for his oil." His "military might was never a threat", but he was "a threat to the dollar". The Bush administration had manufactured a false pretext to go to war to overthrow his regime, generating support for the war "through distortions and flat out misrepresentation of the facts", but "with no evidence of any connection to 9/11, or evidence of weapons of mass destruction". In a short time following the overthrow of Iraq's government, the euro was "abandoned" and "all Iraqi oil sales were carried out in dollars". Now, Iran was posing a new threat "against the petrodollar system", having announced "plans to initiate an oil bourse" in which it would sell oil in euros, not dollars. "If oil markets replace dollars with euros," he warned, "it would in time curtail our ability to continue to print, without restraint, the world's reserve currency." The Congress had once again "bought into the war propaganda against Iran, just as it did against Iraq." Countries that dare to "challenge the system—like Iraq, Iran and Venezuela—become targets of our plans for regime change".

He concluded by saying,

> The economic law that honest exchange demands only things of real value as currency cannot be repealed. The chaos that one day will ensue from our 35-year experiment with worldwide fiat money will require a return to money of real value. We will know that day is

approaching when oil-producing countries demand gold, or its equivalent, for their oil rather than dollars or euros. The sooner the better.[84]

On April 25, 2006, Ron Paul warned of a storm on the horizon, noting that the Fed had "discontinued compiling and reporting the monetary aggregate known as M3", which was "the best description of how quickly the Fed is creating new money and credit"—and yet "Congress makes no demands to receive it." Refusing to release this data, he suggested, was another attempt, along with manipulating interest rates, to fool the market, but this would only work in the short term. "The Fed tries to keep the consumer spending spree going," he explained, "not through hard work and savings, but by creating artificial wealth in stock market bubbles and housing bubbles. When these distortions run their course and are discovered, the corrections will be quite painful."

> The economic harm done by a fiat monetary system is pervasive, dangerous, and unfair. Though runaway inflation is injurious to almost everyone, it is more insidious for certain groups. Once inflation is recognized as a tax, it becomes clear the tax is regressive: penalizing the poor and middle class more than the rich and politically privileged. Price inflation, a consequence of inflating the money supply by the central bank, hits poor and marginal workers first and foremost. It especially penalizes savers, retirees, those on fixed incomes, and anyone who trusts government promises. Small businesses and individual enterprises suffer more than the financial elite, who borrow large sums before the money loses value…. The time for action is now, and it is up to the American people and the U.S. Congress to demand it.[85]

Paul Krugman, by contrast, continued to dismisss any concerns arising from the Fed's inflationary monetary policy. "When it comes to inflation, the main thing we have to fear is fear itself", he wrote, assuring readers that "many economists, including Ben Bernanke, the Federal Reserve chairman, have said that a little bit of inflation—say, 2 percent a year on average—is actually good for the economy." Inflation, in

Krugman's view, as the title of his column declared, was "The Phantom Menace".[86]

In August 2006, Krugman wrote that people were "talking seriously about a possible recession". The economy had grown "fairly fast over the last three years, mainly thanks to a gigantic housing boom", which "led directly to unprecedented spending on home construction" and "allowed consumers to convert rising home values into cash through mortgage refinancing". Instructively, he continued:

> Even optimists generally concede that the housing boom must eventually end, and that consumers will eventually have to start saving again. But the conventional wisdom was that housing would have a "soft landing"—that the boom would taper off gradually, and that other sources of growth would take its place. You might say that the theory was that business investment and exports would stand up as housing stood down.

Once again, Krugman used the literary device of attributing to "conventional wisdom" what was evidently his own thinking, which allowed him to acknowledge that "this theory isn't working" without having to admit that he had been wrong. This time, however, he admitted the role of the Fed in creating the bubble, and reiterated his view that what the Fed needed to do was to replace one bubble with another: "A snarky but accurate description of monetary policy over the past five years is that the Federal Reserve successfully replaced the technology bubble with a housing bubble. But where will the Fed find another bubble?"[87]

Later that month, Krugman wrote that there were "indications that the long-feared housing bust has arrived" and that "the economy as a whole will take a hit."[88] In October, he wrote that "the housing boom became a bubble"—without offering any explanation as to where he drew a distinction between an artificial "boom" and "bubble". He blamed the Fed, but, astoundingly, *not* for having created the bubble! Rather, he criticized, "If anyone is to blame for the current situation, it's Mr. Greenspan who pooh-poohed warnings about an emerging bubble and did nothing to crack down on irresponsible lending."[89]

Krugman thus tossed out a red herring that was transparently designed to shift focus away from the monetary policy he himself had advocated and onto a supposedly under-regulated free market! Apart from his evasion of the already-acknowledged fact that the Fed's low-interest rates had created the housing bubble, this explanation also suffered the fallacy of begging the question. *Why* were banks making irresponsible loans when doing so put them at risk of bankruptcy? *Why* were borrowers taking out loans they wouldn't be able to repay when doing so meant their homes would be foreclosed on? Was it just "irrational exuberance"? Such an explanation is by no means sufficient, and can by no means be reconciled with the fact that the housing bubble was a predictable consequence of lower interest rates. It had, after all, been precisely in order to spur borrowing and spending in the housing sector that Krugman had called for cutting rates in the first place. Thus, when people behaved precisely as he predicted they would, it could hardly be considered "irrational". And how could the Fed have cracked down on lending practices that had been encouraged by federal laws and regulations, and by the implicit promise that financial institutions got into trouble, they would be bailed out by the taxpayers?

On his blog the same day, a reader asked him whether Alan Greenspan had done "the right thing" by "engineering a housing boom". Krugman's response was, "As Paul McCulley of PIMCO remarked when the tech boom crashed, Greenspan needed to create a housing bubble to replace the technology bubble. So within limits he may have done the right thing." His limited criticism was that Greenspan had ignored "the danger signs" and left "a terrible mess for Ben Bernanke."[90]

There are several important points to emphasize here. First, Krugman implicitly acknowledged that the Fed had engineered the housing bubble. Second, to answer in the negative would have meant admitting that he had been wrong to recommend that the Fed do so. Third, he again employed the literary device of attributing to someone else a view that had also been his own. Fourth, saying that the Fed "needed" to create a housing bubble implied an affirmative answer, but then adding that "within limits", the Fed "*may*" have done "the right thing" logically implied the possibility that it may have done the wrong thing. Why the equivocation? Fifth, he repeated the red herring of blaming the Fed for ignoring the bubble, which raises the further paradoxical question of how the Fed could have done the right thing by deliberately creating a housing bubble and yet at the same time erred by ignoring it. The conclusion that he was walking a tightrope—on one hand acknowledging the Fed's role in creating the bubble, but on the other not wishing to admit any error in having advocated that policy—is inescapable.

In March 2007, Krugman commented on how "the collapse of the U.S. housing boom had brought with it widespread defaults on subprime mortgages—loans to home buyers who fail to meet the strictest lending standard." And then hedge funds had leveraged themselves to buy up mortgage-backed securities, borrowing money to invest in these derivatives. "In retrospect," he wrote, "the complacency of investors on the eve of the crisis seems puzzling. Why didn't they see the risks? Well, things always seem clearer with the benefit of hindsight."[91]

Ron Paul, of course, hadn't had "the benefit of hindsight" when repeatedly and precisely predicting this crisis many years in advance. And while Krugman remained stumped, Ron Paul had already explained in his numerous warnings how the Fed's artificially low interest rates sent wrong signals to investors, and how government intervention in the market was incentivizing riskier investments, such as in mortgage-backed securities, which would exacerbate the problem when the housing bubble finally collapsed.

In May 2007, Krugman asked "Why were the bond-rating agencies"—which had been giving mortgage-backed securities the highest "AAA" ratings—"taken in (again), and where were the regulators?"[92] Yet the implication that an unregulated free market was the problem also fails when it comes the rating agencies, which are effectively a government-created cartel.

The few Nationally Recognized Statistical Rating Organizations, such as Standard & Poor's and Moody's, benefit from an oligopoly market structure in which their ratings are recognized by the SEC. The government has to a large extent made these agencies immune from civil and criminal liability for malfeasance, even though the SEC relies on their ratings in making regulatory determinations, which is to say the SEC has outsourced some of its regulatory functions to the ratings agencies oligopoly. A good credit rating thus implies regulatory compliance of the issuer being rated, which pays for its own rating. Traditionally, ratings agencies had sold ratings to investors, but once this cartel was established, they began charging fees to rate issuers of debt, which is where most of their revenue now comes from. In a free market, this apparent conflict of interest might not pose such a hazard, since the agencies would still depend on the credibility of their ratings to remain competitive. However, the same cannot be said when any competition they might otherwise have is eliminated by government decree. Going back to Krugman's question, "Why were the bond-rating agencies taken in (again), and where were the regulators?" The answer is that they *were* the regulators! And this was not the failure of a free market, but of government intervention in the market.[93]

In July 2007, Krugman offered the following explanation of the housing bubble, which explicitly acknowledged the role of low interest rates:

> Back in 2002 and 2003, low interest rates made buying a house look like a very good deal. As people piled into housing, however, prices rose—and people began assuming that they would keep on rising. So the boom fed on itself: borrowers began taking out loans they couldn't really afford and lenders began relaxing their standards.[94]

In August 2007, Krugman noted that there were no buyers for mortgage-backed securities, which "could cause a chain reaction of debt defaults." The origins of this crisis, he said, "lie in the financial follies of the last few years, which in retrospect were as irrational as the dot-com mania." Thus, although Krugman understood the housing bubble to be a predictable consequence of the Fed's low interest rate policy, he was at the same time attempting to deceive his readers into believing that there was just no rational explanation for it. He begged the question: "The housing bubble was only part of it; across the board, people began acting as if risk had disappeared." Why? Krugman had no explanation; it was merely "irrational" human behavior.[95] Illustrating astonishing self-discipline when it came to adhering to his Keynesian ideology, he described the financial crisis as "a serious market failure" and said it "looks to me like a clear case for government intervention".[96] His further answer was to lower interest rates (what else?). He optimistically observed that the Fed's response was to announce "a surprise cut in the discount rate, the rate at which it lends money to banks".[97]

In October 2007, Krugman asked the bold question, "why was nothing done to head off this disaster?" His answer was that it was a consequence of "the laissez-faire ideologues ruling Washington" and the belief "that government is always the problem, never the solution, that regulation is always a bad thing", and "that unregulated financial markets would take care of themselves". In short, the problem had been a "radical deregulation of financial markets."[98] In another column, he wrote that "the problem was ideological: policy makers, committed to the view that the market is always right, simply ignored the warning signs."[99] Krugman did not completely absolve the Fed of responsibility; he blamed it once more for failing "to regulate lending".[100]

Ron Paul was arguing the opposite, cautioning that more regulation would not solve the problem, because it did not address the fundamental causes of the housing bubble:

> Further regulation of the banking sector, of mortgage brokers, mortgage lenders, or credit rating agencies will fail to improve the current situation, and will do nothing to prevent future real estate bubbles. Any proposed solutions which fail to take into account the economic intervention that laid the ground for the bubble are merely window dressing, and will not ease the suffering of millions of American homeowners. I urge my colleagues to strike at the root of the problem and address the Federal Reserve's inflationary monetary policy.[101]

The housing bubble had not been a consequence of an unregulated free market, Ron Paul observed. On the contrary, "For years the federal government has made it one of its prime aims to encourage homeownership among people who otherwise would not be able to afford homes." In addition to the special privileges and implicit government backing afforded to Fannie Mae and Freddie Mac,

> Legislation such as the Zero Downpayment Act and the misnamed American Dream Downpayment Act made it possible for people who could not afford down payments on houses to receive assistance from the federal government, or even to pay no down payment at all, courtesy of the taxpayers. The requirement of a down payment has always helped to ascertain the ability of a buyer to pay off a mortgage. It requires the buyer to show hard work and thrift, the ability to delay present consumption in order to make a larger acquisition in the future.

When this requirement is minimized or eliminated, you introduce a new class of homebuyers, people who are unable to budget and save for the purchase of a home, or who should wait for a few years until they have saved enough to purchase a home. Federal policies have encouraged investors, lenders, and brokers to cater to these people, so it is no surprise that market actors came up with ever more sophisticated means of bringing these people into the real estate market.

Most importantly, the Fed's inflationary monetary policy had provided the cheap credit that drove the housing bubble. "It is time that the federal government get out of the housing business", he proclaimed. "Through our interventionist legislation we have caused the boom and bust, and any attempts at reform that fail to address the causes of our current problem will only sow the seeds for the next bubble."[102]

Know them by their fruits

On June 17, 2009, Paul Krugman responded to criticisms that he had called for low interest rates to create housing bubble with a blog post titled, "And I was on the grassy knoll, too"—the implication being that his critics were loony conspiracy theorists, a tactic by which he attempted to obfuscate the legitimacy of the criticism throughout his post:

> One of the funny aspects of being a somewhat, um, forceful writer is that I'm regularly accused of all sorts of villainy. I was personally responsible for the demise of Enron; my nonexistent son worked for Hillary; etc. The latest seems to be that I called for the creation of a housing bubble—in fact, the bubble is my fault! The claim seems to be based on this piece. ["Dubya's Double Dip?" *New York Times*, August 2, 2002] Guys, read it again. It wasn't a piece of policy advocacy, it was just economic analysis. What I said was that the only way the Fed could get traction would be if it could inflate a housing bubble. And that's just what happened.[103]

By conjoining the spurious charge that the bubble was his "fault" with the legitimate criticism that he had called for it, he could create the strawman argument that since he hadn't personally created the bubble (and whoever claimed that?), therefore his critics were not only wrong, but so bizarre in their criticism that they must be delusional. The fact remained that he had *repeatedly* argued in favor of artificially low interest rates *specifically* in order to spur a housing boom. As for his denial that this had been "just economic analysis" and not "policy advocacy", is it possible that he did not know the meaning of the noun "advocacy", meaning "supporting a cause or proposal", or the verb "advocate", meaning "to plead in favor of"?[104]

When Krugman wrote, "let's have at least one more rate cut, please" (May 2, 2001), he was not advocating cutting interest rates? When he wrote that creating a demand for "housing, which is highly sensitive to interest rates, could help lead a recovery" (August 14, 2001), he was not advocating lowering interest rates to create demand for housing? When he expressed that he was "a little depressed" because "long-term rates haven't fallen enough to produce a boom" in housing (August 2, 2001), it did not qualify as advocacy for cutting interest rates to spur a housing boom? When he wrote that, to "reflate the economy", the Fed had to increase demand and that "housing, which is highly sensitive to interest rates, could help lead a recovery" (August 14, 2001), he wasn't advocating that the Fed cut interest rates? It was not policy advocacy when he wrote that "economic policy should encourage other spending to offset the temporary slump in business investment. Low interest rates, which promote spending on housing and other durable goods, are the main answer" (October 7, 2001)? It would be superfluous to continue. The fact is that Krugman *did* advocate a policy of creating a housing bubble to replace the dot-com bubble, his disingenuous protests to the contrary notwithstanding.

Humorously, one commenter on Krugman's blog post replied with a link to an interview Krugman had given to a Spanish TV channel just a few months before. In the interview, Krugman said, "To be honest, a new bubble now would help us out a lot even if we paid for it later. This is a really good time for a bubble.... There was a headline in a satirical newspaper [*The Onion*] in the U.S. last summer that said, 'The nation demands a new bubble to invest in'. And that's pretty much right."[105] Krugman's record is clear and unambiguous. "Guys, read it again," indeed!

Krugman continued to deflect blame away from the policy course he himself had advocated in the aftermath of the financial crisis, and thus away from the role the Fed had played in creating the housing bubble. In a September 6, 2009 article for the *Times* titled "How Did Economists Get It So Wrong?" Krugman remarked that "Few economists saw our current crisis coming," but continued on to blame this "predictive failure" and "blindness" on "most economists" clinging to "a vision of capitalism as a perfect or nearly perfect system". Economists had failed to learn lessons from history and "turned a blind eye to the limitations of human rationality that often lead to bubbles and busts". Economists had ignored "the imperfections of markets" and now "have to acknowledge the importance of irrational and often unpredictable behavior".[106]

But, again, how could he call the consequence of a housing bubble "unpredictable" when increased investment in housing was precisely the outcome he had *hoped* would occur as a consequence of low interest rates? And when the market responded as Krugman had *hoped* it would, how can this then be attributed to "irrational" human behavior? And if the housing bubble was a consequence of the Fed's *interference* in the free market by *artificially* keeping interest rates low, how then could "capitalism" and "the imperfections of markets" be identified as the chief culprit? His fallacies were glaring, and it is highly ironic that he could attribute to any *other* economists a "blindness" and willingness to "turn a blind eye" due to adherence to ideology.

Again on April 5, 2010, Krugman attempted to exonerate himself and obfuscate his own record, writing in his blog that people were taking his earlier remarks calling for a housing boom "out-of-context":

> So did I call for a bubble? The quote comes from this 2002 piece ["Dubya's Double Dip?" *New York Times*, August 2, 2002], in which I was pessimistic about the Fed's ability to generate a sustained economy. If you read it in context, you'll see that I wasn't calling for a bubble— I was talking about the limits to the Fed's powers, saying that the only way Greenspan could achieve recovery would be if he were able to create a new bubble, which is NOT the same thing as saying that this was a good idea. Of course, I know that this explanation won't keep the haters from pulling up the same quote out of context, over and over.

Instructively, Krugman admitted, "But did I call for low interest rates? Yes." But, he argued, that "doesn't make me someone who deliberately sought a bubble."[107]

Strictly speaking, that is logically true. Yet the fact of the matter remained that he had explicitly stated that the goal of the policy he advocated should be to create a housing bubble. His disingenuousness here is highly instructive, and provides insights into his overall revisionist analysis of the main causes of the financial crisis. The nonsensicalness of the implied argument that he had *not* thought the Fed should do what he admittedly believed was "the only way" to "achieve recovery" is self-evident; he might just as well have tried to deny that he had thought an economic recovery would be a good idea. It was another absurd denial, and the context of the remark was not on his side. But, of course, anyone who dared to point out Krugman's own words to him was dismissed as merely a "hater".

Krugman again argued in the *New York Review of Books* in September 2010 that the Fed had had no choice but to lower interest rates following the collapse of the dot-com bubble. "It's hard to see," he wrote, "even in retrospect, how the Fed could have justified not keeping rates low for an extended period." However, now his argument was that "it would be wrong to attribute the real estate bubble wholly, or even in large part, to misguided monetary policy."[108]

Yet how could Krugman reconcile his argument here that the Fed was not "wholly, or even in large part" responsible for creating the housing bubble with his earlier arguments that the Fed should lower interest rates to spur investment in housing? How could he reconcile this argument with his earlier statement that "Millions of Americans have decided that low interest rates offer a good opportunity to refinance their homes or buy new ones" (May 2, 2001)? Or with his observation that "those 11 interest rate cuts in 2001 fueled a boom both in housing purchases and in mortgage refinancing" (October 1, 2002)? Or with his acknowledgment that it had been "the Fed's dramatic interest rate cuts" that had "helped keep housing strong" (December 28, 2001)? Or his statement, "Repeated interest rate cuts encouraged families to buy new houses and refinance their mortgages" (December 22, 2002)? Or his remark that "Mortgage rates did indeed fall briefly to historic lows, extending the home-buying and refinancing boom that has helped keep the economy's head above water" (July 25, 2003)? Or, "Low interest rates … have been crucial to America's housing boom" (May 20, 2005)? Or, "interest rate cuts led to soaring home prices, which led in turn not just to a construction boom but to high consumer spending, because homeowners used mortgage refinancing to go deeper into debt"(May 25, 2005)? Or, "A snarky but accurate description of monetary policy over the past five years is that the Federal Reserve successfully replaced the technology bubble with a housing bubble" (August 7, 2006)? Or, "Back in 2002 and 2003, low interest rates made buying a house look like a very good deal. As people piled into housing, however, prices rose—and people began assuming that they would keep on rising. So the boom fed on itself" (July 27, 2007)?

What can explain Krugman's self-contradictions? When he thought the housing bubble was a good thing, the road to recovery, he was all for it, lavishing the Fed with praise for single-handedly rescuing the economy from the much more painful recession that otherwise would have occurred without it. Once the devastating consequences of the housing bubble became clear, however, he changed his story, denying that he had ever called for a bubble and even denying that the Fed was responsible for having created it.

As the crisis wore on, Krugman continued to warn *against* cutting government spending, arguing that more spending was needed for the government to create jobs.[109] In August 2011, he wrote, "To turn this disaster around, a lot of people are going to have to admit, to themselves at least, that they've been wrong and need to change their priorities, right away." Krugman, of course, excluded himself. *He* was always right. Part of the problem, in his view, was that "Consumers, still burdened by the debt that they ran up during the housing bubble, aren't ready to spend." How to solve that? Inflation! Encouraging *more* debt! He criticized the Fed for being "more concerned with hypothetical inflation than with real unemployment, partly because it let itself be intimidated by the Ron Paul types." So in Krugman's new calculus, the Fed bore no blame for creating a housing bubble with artificially low interest rates or for being "intimidated" into implementing that policy by Paul Krugman types. Better to blame the "Ron Paul types" whose warnings were ignored and whose policy prescriptions were never implemented.[110]

His continued advocacy for still further inflation included the argument that a weaker dollar would boost exports. He remarked that "sensible policy makers have long known that sometimes a weaker currency means a stronger economy."[111] So if you, dear mortal reader, were of the opinion that a strong currency was the mark of a healthy economy, you are fooling yourself with nonsense the more intelligent and enlightened minds of the world know to be a delusion.

Krugman again had the audacity to aim criticism at Ron Paul in December 2011:

> Unfortunately, Mr. Paul has maintained his consistency by ignoring reality, clinging to his ideology even as the facts have demonstrated that ideology's wrongness....

Mr. Paul identifies himself as a believer in "Austrian" economics—a doctrine that it goes without saying rejects John Maynard Keynes.... For Austrians see "fiat money," money that is just printed without being backed by gold, as the root of all economic evil, which means that they fiercely oppose the kind of monetary expansion ... carried out by Ben Bernanke this time around....

Austrians, and for that matter many right-leaning economists, were sure about what would happen as a result: There would be devastating inflation....

So here we are, three years later. How's it going? Inflation has fluctuated, but, at the end of the day, consumer prices have risen just 4.5 percent, meaning an average annual inflation rate of only 1.5 percent. Who could have predicted that printing so much money would cause so little inflation? Well, I could. And did. And so did others who understood the Keynesian economics Mr. Paul reviles. But Mr. Paul's supporters continue to claim, somehow, that he has been right about everything.... Now, it's still very unlikely that Ron Paul will become president. But, as I said, his economic doctrine has, in effect, become the official G.O.P. line, despite having been proved utterly wrong by events. And what will happen if that doctrine actually ends up being put into action? Great Depression, here we come.[112]

The suggestion that Ron Paul had "been proved utterly wrong by events" would seem to be a case of classic psychological projection, and indicative of an extreme self-delusion. It's enough to note that Krugman here employs numerous fallacies. If Ron Paul had been wrong about the effects of inflation, it would not follow that therefore the Austrian school had "been proved utterly wrong". That is, if it *had* been proven wrong on one point, that wouldn't mean it had been wrong on everything else. In addition to being a *non sequitur*, this argument was also a red herring. Krugman was transparently attempting to divert attention away from the fact that the "Austrians" had *correctly* predicted the housing bubble and its disastrous economic consequences. It was also a strawman, for simple fact of the matter that Ron Paul *hadn't* warned of "devastating inflation" *with inflation defined as a rise in prices in consumer goods*. Krugman was thus guilty either of ignorance or dishonesty.

While Krugman characterized Ron Paul as having warned of "devastating inflation" and pointed to an annual inflation rate of "only 1.5 percent" as proof that Ron Paul was wrong, in fact the latest CPI figure available to him at the time was a 3.4 percent increase over 12 months, more than double what Krugman asserted to be the annual inflation rate.[113]

More importantly, one must recall that Ron Paul had explicitly *rejected* Krugman's own definition of inflation as a rise in prices of consumer goods. He rather defined inflation as an increase in the money supply, pointing out that rising prices was a *consequence* of inflation. Krugman acknowledged in the same article that "there has, indeed, been a huge expansion of the monetary base", thus admitting that there had indeed been "huge" inflation as "Austrians" defined it![114]

Furthermore, Ron Paul had argued that the government's Consumer Price Index (CPI) was *not* an accurate measure of rising prices. For example, the current methodology of calculating the CPI understates by half what it would be using pre-1990 methodology. As John Williams of ShadowStats.com has explained, the CPI used to be "measured using the costs of a fixed basket of goods", but later changes in methodology were based on the argument

> that when steak got too expensive, the consumer would substitute hamburger for the steak, and that the inflation measure should reflect the costs tied to buying hamburger versus steak, instead of steak versus steak. Of course, replacing hamburger for steak in the calculations would reduce the inflation rate, but it represented the rate of inflation in terms of maintaining a declining standard of living. Cost of living was being replaced by the cost of survival. The old system told you how much you had to increase your income in order to keep buying steak. The new system promised you hamburger, and then dog food, perhaps, after that.[115]

Krugman must also certainly have been aware that U.S. banks were keeping excess reserves rather than fully loaning up to the minimal fractional-reserve requirement. Surely he was aware that the Fed was paying banks interest on their excess reserves, thus effectively paying them *not* to lend money.[116] This policy was thus preventing the banks from further inflating the money supply through the magic of fractional-reserve banking, which had also reduced the effects of the Fed's expansion of the monetary base on consumer goods prices.

Additionally, Ron Paul had explained that rising prices for consumer goods was only one of many possible consequence of inflation. It is useful to recall his statement that "those who claim" that "we have no inflation to fear" "define inflation as rising consumer and producer prices", but "the free market definition of inflation is the increase in the supply of money and credit", which "can cause great harm without significantly affecting government price indices. The excess credit may well go into stock market and real estate speculation" (February 14, 2001). We may also recall his remark that "significant price increases need not exist for monetary inflation to place a hardship on the economy" (September 6, 2001).

Ron Paul had elucidated how inflation did not necessarily result in a uniform rise in prices throughout the economy, but could result in rising costs in one sector over another, such as in capital rather than consumer goods. It encouraged spending rather than saving. It lowered interest rates and sent wrong signals to entrepreneurs and investors about the pool of capital available for longer-term projects. It helped the rich who receive the money first and are able to spend it before prices rise, while harming members of the poor and middle class who had tried to save. It weakened the dollar, which would ultimately result in foreign investors losing confidence and ceasing to purchase U.S. debt, which would push interest rates upward and cause the government to be unable to finance its interest-bearing debt obligations. In addition, the U.S., as the issuer of the world's reserve currency, benefited from being able to export its inflation, with other nations racing to debase their currencies to keep their exports competitive.

In sum, Krugman's argument that inflation remained "The Phantom Menace", as he had earlier called it, and that Austrian economics had somehow been debunked based on a single government statistic falls flat on its face, illustrating a rather pathetic insistence that he had been right and Ron Paul wrong.

But Paul Krugman persisted in his delusions, continuing to argue that the reason there was no economic recovery was because the government just wasn't spending enough to create jobs. He even repeated his belief that "even useless spending can be expansionary"![117]

Incredibly, the lesson he took away from government's response to the housing bubble was that "Keynes Was Right". He asserted that "Slashing government spending in a depressed economy depresses the economy further" and that "austerity" had failed—even though there *were* no spending cuts; in fact, the government had projected massive *increases* in spending over the next decade (a fact he must certainly have been aware of, but chose not to disclose to his readers, for the obvious reason).[118] He noted that the Obama administration had passed a "stimulus package" that had failed to produce the jobs it had promised, but this was merely because it "was much too small"—an argument that also unwittingly illustrated the absurdity of blaming "austerity" when it had so obviously not been tried.

"In declaring Keynesian economics vindicated", Krugman boasted, "I am, of course, at odds with conventional wisdom." Since when had he become a maverick? What happened to his view that "as a result of the Keynesian revolution" it became "obvious to everyone ... that the problem during a slump is too little spending" (July 18, 2001)? Had his own "conventional wisdom" taken a 180 degree turn since the housing bubble had collapsed? If so, how did one explain the Fed's monetary expansion, the ever-increasing government spending, the "stimulus" plans, the bailouts, etc.? Blaming "austerity" for the nation's persisting economic problems was as ludicrous as blaming the free market for the housing bubble—but choosing to believe such delusions were the only means by which Krugman could continue to cling to his own Keynesian ideology.

Conclusion

So who was the true prophet, and who the false? Whose predictions came true? While Paul Krugman remained unconvinced of the existence of the dot-com bubble and dismissed fears of a recession with the argument that the Federal Reserve could easily prevent one by lowering interest rates, Ron Paul correctly predicted that the bubble would burst, resulting in an inevitable recession. While Paul Krugman advocated a monetary policy of maintaining artificially low interest rates in order to manufacture a boom in housing, Ron Paul correctly predicted that this policy would create a housing bubble that would pose a threat not only to the U.S. but to the global economy when it burst, as it ultimately must do.

There's just no contest. Krugman was continuously wrong, and Ron Paul was consistently correct. While Krugman regularly equivocated and offered incoherent and self-contradictory explanations in an attempt to divert attention away from the role of the policy he had advocated in creating the housing bubble, Ron Paul's message for over a decade remained perfectly consistent in warning against that same policy.

Inasmuch as each man represents an opposing school of economic thought, the further corollary seems incontrovertible that the financial crisis has shown Keynesianism to be a thoroughly bankrupt school of economic thought. It has at the same time vindicated proponents of the Austrian school and attested to the cogency of its business cycle theory.

Appendix: Warnings for the Future

Ron Paul has continued to warn against the economic policies of the government and Federal Reserve. It follows from the examination of his record that Americans would be wise to heed him.

On February 27, 2008, Ron Paul spoke against further government intervention in the market, warning that the proposals to deal with the bust constituted a "moral hazard", including calls for the government to buy up existing mortgages that could potentially default, placing the burden on the American taxpayers and perpetuating the instability of the housing market:

> The Congress has, over the past decades, relentlessly pushed for increased rates of homeownership among people who have always been viewed by the market as poor credit risks. Various means and incentives have been used by the government, but behind all the actions of lenders has been an implicit belief in a federal bailout in the event of a crisis.
>
> What all of these proposed bailouts fail to mention is the moral hazard to which bailouts lead. If the federal government bails out banks, investors, or homeowners, the lessons of sound investment and fiscal discipline will not take hold. We can see this in the financial markets in

the boom and bust of the business cycle. The Fed's manipulation of interest rates results in malinvestment which, when it is discovered, leads to economic contraction and liquidation of malinvested resources. But the Fed never allows a complete shakeout, so that before a return to a sound market can occur, the Fed has already bailed out numerous market participants by undertaking another bout of loose money before the effects of the last business cycle have worked their way through the economy.

Many market actors therefore continue to undertake risky investments and expect that in the future, if their investments go south, that the Fed would and should intervene by creating more money and credit. The result of these bailouts is that each successive recession runs the risk of becoming larger and more severe, requiring a stronger reaction by the Fed. Eventually, however, the Fed begins to run out of room in which to maneuver, a problem we are facing today.

I urge my colleagues to resist the temptation to call for easy fixes in the form of bailouts. If we fail to address and stem the problem of moral hazard, we are doomed to experience repeated severe economic crises.[119]

On July 24, 2008, he again spoke out against the "implicit government guarantee of Fannie Mae and Freddie Mac", calling for an end in "government support for Fannie and Freddie and repealing all laws that interfere in housing." The bursting of the housing bubble had proven the Austrian economists correct, he said, but instead of heeding its lessons, the Congress was reacting by "increasing the level of government intervention in the housing market. This is the equivalent of giving a drug addict another fix, which will only make the necessary withdrawal more painful."[120]

"Unfortunately," Ron Paul wrote in September 2008, after the government had begun its bailouts of troubled financial institutions, "the government's preferred solution to the crisis is the very thing that got us into this mess in the first place: government intervention." The cause of

Appendix: Warnings for the Future

==the housing bubble, Ron Paul explained, had not been the free market, but, on the contrary, government intervention in the market:==

> Ever since the 1930s, the federal government has involved itself deeply in housing policy and developed numerous programs to encourage homebuilding and homeownership. Government-sponsored enterprises Fannie Mae and Freddie Mac were able to obtain a monopoly position in the mortgage market, especially the mortgage-backed securities market, because of the advantages bestowed upon them by the federal government. Laws passed by Congress such as the Community Reinvestment Act required banks to make loans to previously underserved segments of their communities, thus forcing banks to lend to people who normally would be rejected as bad credit risks.

Such intervention had contributed to the housing bubble.

Continuing, Ron Paul explained how the bust was the inevitable consequence of the artificially created boom:

> Because the boom comes about from an increase in the supply of money and not from demand from consumers, the result is malinvestment, a misallocation of resources into sectors in which there is insufficient demand. In this case, this manifested itself in overbuilding in real estate. When builders realize they have overbuilt and have too many houses to sell, too many apartments to rent, or too much commercial real estate to lease, they seek to recoup as much of their money as possible, even if it means lowering prices drastically. This lowering of prices brings the economy back into balance, equalizing supply and demand. This economic adjustment means, however, that there are some winners—in this case, those who can again find affordable housing without the need for creative mortgage products—and some losers, builders and other sectors connected to real estate that suffer setbacks.

But now, rather than allowing the market to determine prices, the government was again trying to intervene and undertaking "measures to keep prices artificially inflated." The bailouts were simply more of the same kind of government intervention in the market that had helped to create the crisis in the first place:

> I am afraid that policymakers today have not learned the lesson that prices must adjust to economic reality. The bailout of Fannie and Freddie, the purchase of AIG, and the latest multi-hundred billion dollar Treasury scheme all have one thing in common: They seek to prevent the liquidation of bad debt and worthless assets at market prices, and instead try to prop up those markets and keep those assets trading at prices far in excess of what any buyer would be willing to pay. Additionally, the government's actions encourage moral hazard of the worst sort. Now that the precedent has been set, the likelihood of financial institutions to engage in riskier investment schemes is increased, because they now know that an investment position so overextended as to threaten the stability of the financial system will result in a government bailout and purchase of worthless, illiquid assets. Using trillions of dollars of taxpayer money to purchase illusory short-term security, the government is actually ensuring even greater instability in the financial system in the long term.

> The solution to the problem is to end government meddling in the market. Government intervention leads to distortions in the market, and government reacts to each distortion by enacting new laws and regulations, which create their own distortions, and so on, *ad infinitum*. It is time this process is put to an end. But the government cannot just sit back idly and let the bust occur. It must actively roll back stifling laws and regulations that allowed the boom to form in the first place. The government must divorce itself of the albatross of Fannie and Freddie, balance and drastically decrease the size of the federal budget, and reduce onerous regulations on banks and credit unions that lead to structural rigidity in the financial sector. Until the big-government apologists realize the error of their ways, and

Appendix: Warnings for the Future

until vocal free-market advocates act in a manner which buttresses their rhetoric, I am afraid we are headed for a rough ride.[121]

As the government contemplated the $700 billion Troubled Asset Relief Program (TARP), Ron Paul on September 24, 2008 spoke out against the plan to "purchase overvalued or worthless assets and hold them in the unrealistic hope that at some point in the next few decades, someone might be willing to purchase them." In addition:

> One of the perverse effects of this bailout proposal is that the worst-performing firms, and those who interjected themselves most deeply into mortgage-backed securities, credit default swaps, and special investment vehicles will be those who benefit the most from this bailout.... This creates a dangerous moral hazard, as the precedent of bailing out reckless lending will lead to even more reckless lending and irresponsible behavior on the part of financial firms in the future.... That we have come to a point where outright purchases of private sector companies is not only proposed but accepted by many who claim to be defenders of free markets bodes ill for the future of American society.... The housing bubble has burst, unemployment is on the rise, and the dollar weakens every day. Unfortunately our leaders have failed to learn from the mistakes of previous generations and continue to lead us down the road toward economic ruin.[122]

Again the same day he warned:

> This $700 billion bailout will only increase that debt, and increase the amount of money we pay merely to service the interest on that debt. The end result of this is higher taxes on our children and grandchildren, and the full-scale destruction of the dollar. The only viable solution to this financial crisis is to keep the government from intervening any further. The Federal Reserve has already loaned hundreds of billions of dollars through its numerous lending facilities, and the Congress has passed

> legislation authorizing further hundreds of billions of dollars to bail out Fannie and Freddie, yet each successive crisis event seems to be advertised as larger and more severe than the previous one. It is time that this Congress put its foot down, reject the administration's proposal, and allow the bust to work itself out so that our economic hangover is not as severe as it might otherwise be.[123]

He warned on September 29, 2008, "Monetary reform will eventually come, but, unfortunately, Congress' actions this week make it more likely the reform will come under dire circumstances, such as the midst of a worldwide collapse of the dollar. The question then will be how much of our liberties will be sacrificed in the process."[124]

Again on October 3, 2008, he repeated his warning that the bailouts presented a "moral hazard" by benefiting the "worst performing financial services firms". He asked his fellow Congressmen,

> What incentive do Wall Street firms or any other large concerns have to make sound financial decisions, now that they see the federal government bailing out private companies to the tune of trillions of dollars? As Congress did with the legislation authorizing the Fannie and Freddie bailout, it proposes a solution that exacerbates and encourages the problematic behavior that led to this crisis in the first place.

> With deposit insurance increasing to $250,000 and banks able to set their reserves to zero, we will undoubtedly see future increases in unsound lending. No one in our society seems to understand that wealth is not created by government fiat, is not created by banks, and is not created through the manipulation of interest rates and provision of easy credit. A debt-based society cannot prosper and is doomed to fail, as debts must either be defaulted on or repaid, neither resolution of which presents this country with a pleasant view of the future. True wealth can only come about through savings, the deferral of present consumption in order to provide for a higher level of future

consumption. Instead, our government through its own behavior and through its policies encourages us to live beyond our means, reducing existing capital and mortgaging our future to pay for present consumption.

The money for this bailout does not just materialize out of thin air. The entire burden will be borne by the taxpayers, not now, because that is politically unacceptable, but in the future. This bailout will be paid for through the issuance of debt which we can only hope will be purchased by foreign creditors. The interest payments on that debt, which already take up a sizeable portion of federal expenditures, will rise, and our children and grandchildren will be burdened with increased taxes in order to pay that increased debt.

As usual, Congress has shown itself to be reactive rather than proactive. For years, many people have been warning about the housing bubble and the inevitable bust. Congress ignored the impending storm, and responded to this crisis with a poorly thought-out piece of legislation that will only further harm the economy. We ought to be ashamed.[125]

On November 20, 2008, Ron Paul remarked:

Although it is obvious that the Keynesians were all wrong and interventionism and central economic planning don't work, whom are we listening to for advice on getting us out of this mess? Unfortunately, it's the Keynesians, the socialists, and big-government proponents. Who's being ignored? The Austrian free-market economists—the very ones who predicted not only the Great Depression, but the calamity we're dealing with today. If the crisis was predictable and is explainable, why did no one listen?

...A country cannot forever depend on a central bank to keep the economy afloat and the currency functionable through constant acceleration of money supply growth. Eventually the laws of economics will overrule the politicians, the bureaucrats and the central bankers. The system will fail to respond unless the excess debt and malinvestment is liquidated. If it goes too far and the wild extravagance is not arrested, runaway inflation will result, and an entirely new currency will be required to restore growth and reasonable political stability. The choice we face is ominous: We either accept world-wide authoritarian government holding together a flawed system, *or* we restore the principles of the Constitution, limit government power, restore commodity money without a Federal Reserve system, reject world government, and promote the cause of peace by protecting liberty equally for all persons. Freedom is the answer.[126]

On February 25, 2009, he again cautioned that "Inflation has been used to pay for all wars and empires. And they all end badly." In addition, "There is no legal authority to operate such a monetary system. So let's stop it. Let's restore a policy of prosperity, peace, and liberty. The time has come. Let's End the Fed."[127] He introduced the Federal Reserve Transparency Act on February 26, 2009, commenting:

> Throughout its nearly 100-year history, the Federal Reserve has presided over the near-complete destruction of the United States dollar. Since 1913 the dollar has lost over 95% of its purchasing power, aided and abetted by the Federal Reserve's loose monetary policy. How long will we as a Congress stand idly by while hard-working Americans see their savings eaten away by inflation?

The Fed "always operated in the shadows, without sufficient scrutiny or oversight of its operations", and could even "enter into agreements with foreign central banks and foreign governments" without any oversight. In the face of "hundreds of billions of dollars of currency swaps" the Fed was undertaking,

> the Fed's negotiations with the European Central Bank, the Bank of International Settlements, and other institutions should face increased scrutiny, most especially because of their significant effect on foreign policy. If the

Appendix: Warnings for the Future

State Department were able to do this, it would be characterized as a rogue agency and brought to heel, and if a private individual did this he might face prosecution under the Logan Act, yet the Fed avoids both fates.[128]

On February 9, 2011, commented on the "dual mandate" of the Fed to keep prices stable and maximize unemployment, which was influenced by Keynesian economics and "relies on the idea that a handful of experts can successfully steer the American economy and create economic growth. This has forced upon us an interventionist monetary policy that believes that creation of money out of thin air is the cure for all that ails us." The Fed had "failed miserably" on its first mandate. "According to the government's own CPI calculators," he noted "it takes $2.65 today to purchase what cost one dollar in 1980. And since its creation in 1913, the Federal Reserve has presided over a 98% decline in the dollar's purchasing power." As for its second mandate, "The stagflation of the 1970s should have taught us this lesson already. The Federal Reserve's loose monetary policy, rather than leading to a tradeoff between jobs and inflation, instead led to both high inflation and high unemployment. Hopefully we will learn the lesson this time around." He added:

> Consider that we had a $700 billion TARP program, nearly $1 trillion in stimulus spending, a government takeover of General Motors, and hundreds of billions of dollars of guarantees to Fannie Mae, Freddie Mac, HUD, FDIC, etc. On top of those programs the Federal Reserve has provided over $4 trillion worth of assistance over the past few years through its credit facilities, purchases of mortgage-backed securities, and now its second round of quantitative easing. Yet even after all these trillions of dollars of spending and bailouts, total nonfarm payroll employment is still seven million jobs lower than it was before this crisis began. Since employment levels bottomed out last year, the government reports that roughly one million jobs have been created.
>
> This means that each job created has cost upwards of five million dollars. We probably would have been better off

just printing out these trillions of dollars and throwing them out the window of a helicopter.

But above all, he said, "it is the effects of monetary policy itself that cause the boom and bust of the business cycle that leads to swings in the unemployment rate." He elaborated:

> By lowering interest rates through its loose monetary policy, the Fed spurs investment in long-term projects that would not be profitable at market-determined interest rates. The signal to businesses is that consumers are increasing savings and deferring consumption in order to consume more capital-intensive [*sic*] more in the future. If the Fed-mandated interest rate is in fact lower than the market interest rate, the reality is that consumer preferences between consumption and savings have not changed, *but businesses act as though they have*. The result of lower interest rates is an economic boom which manifests itself as a bubble.
>
> Everything seems to go well for a while until businesses realize that they cannot sell their newly-built houses, their inventories of iron ore, or their new cars. Low interest rates have spurred production, but because the low interest rates resulted from Fed intervention and not through changes in consumption patterns, the result is overcapacity. Resources have been "malinvested," directed into sectors of the economy which are not truly in demand from consumers. These resources must be liquidated, and this is the corresponding bursting of the bubble. Until these resources are redirected, often with great economic pain for all involved, true economic recovery cannot begin.
>
> Labor is one of these resources that can be malinvested. As inflation rises due to the Fed's monetary intervention, real wage rates decrease, increasing the demand for labor and leading to lower unemployment. Sectors into which this new money flows see hiring increases, as we recently saw in financial services, mortgage lending, and

Appendix: Warnings for the Future

construction during the housing boom. When the bust comes, however, these workers end up being laid off. They find it difficult to find employment in other industries due to an inability to sell their houses and move, or to retrain for a new skilled labor position, or for any number of other reasons. However, the result of that initial meddling in monetary policy is an eventual increase in the unemployment rate.

We find ourselves now in the midst of the worst economic crisis in decades. Unemployment remains persistently high, and the United States cannot afford increased meddling by the Federal Reserve. Over $4 trillion in bailout facilities and outright debt monetization, combined with interest rates near zero for over two years, have not and will not contribute to increased employment. I shudder to think of what the Fed might do if the unemployment rate were to continue to increase.

By falsely diagnosing the cause of the crisis, the Fed's solution is fatally flawed. What is needed is liquidation of debt and of malinvested resources. Pumping money into the same sectors that have just crashed merely prolongs the crisis and ensures that the day of financial reckoning that eventually will come will be far more severe than otherwise. Until we learn the lesson that jobs are produced through real savings and investment and not through the creation of new money, we are doomed to repeat this boom and bust cycle.[129]

On May 11, 2011, Ron Paul stated that the Fed was increasingly acting as "the buyer of last resort for U.S. Treasury debt". The next step, history teaches, is severe inflation, which had only been curtailed because "the Fed has managed to keep the monetary base increases in check by paying interest on excess reserves held by banks. If these excess reserves begin to be loaned out, however, all bets are off." He warned against the ever-increasing government spending:

We are told that Congress must raise the debt ceiling limit or else the financial markets and the U.S. economy will suffer great harm. In reality, raising the debt ceiling will allow the government to continue its fiscal profligacy. Fed financed deficits will continue; foreign investors will continue to divest their holdings of Treasury securities; the Fed will be forced to monetize new debt issuances, and prices will continue to rise as the standard of living of the average American continues to plummet. If we have learned anything from history, we should know that printing money out of thin air cannot lead to prosperity. It can only lead to penury.[130]

On July 26, 2011, Ron Paul warned:

Like many critics of the Fed's monetary policy, I fear that quantitative easing will soon return. Despite what we hear from the cheerleaders in government and in the media, the economy remains in a complete shambles. Unemployment remains high and seven million jobs lost during the recession have yet to be regained. The Federal Reserve has kept interest rates at or near zero for over two and a half years and pumped trillions of dollars into the banking system in a vain attempt to revive the economy. Yet even now after the failure of the zero interest rate policy (ZIRP) and quantitative easing have become readily apparent, we still hear calls for more stimulus, more easing, more loose money. Like any other government program, the solution for failure is to throw more money at the problem, never mind the fact that throwing more bad money after good in such instances has never succeeded.

Reading the press releases from the Federal Open Market Committee (FOMC) we see that the FOMC intends to keep interest rates at a low level for an extended period. Chairman Bernanke has hinted at a further round of quantitative easing, the effects of which will undoubtedly be calamitous. Moneyholders seek a return on their holdings, and in an era of near-zero interest courtesy of the Fed, saving makes no sense. Combined with the still-shaky condition of the banking and financial sector, it is not surprising that much of the recently-created easy money has flowed into tangibles such as agricultural commodities, metals, and land. Rather than allowing the housing bubble to burst, overall prices to return to normal and overleveraged banks to break up, the Fed has thrown more fuel onto the fire and created the conditions for an even larger bubble that will eventually burst.

The Fed's easy money policy has also enabled the federal government to increase its total debt by 56% since 2008, an increase of over $5 trillion. Thanks to the Fed driving down interest rates and purchasing debt as fast as the Treasury has issued it, the federal government faces a crunch not only in terms of running up against the debt ceiling, but also in the structure of the debt. Large amounts of short-term debt are coming due in a short period of time. ZIRP and quantitative easing cannot hold down interest rates forever, as at some point investors will rebel and insist on higher interest rates for US debt. At this point this maturing debt will either have to be paid off or rolled over at higher interest rates, both of which will be very costly for taxpayers....

Chairman Bernanke's predecessor Alan Greenspan fueled the dot-com bubble and attempted to stave off its collapse by resorting to one percent interest rates. That created the housing bubble whose collapse Chairman Bernanke is attempting to stymie through zero percent interest and massive quantitative easing. The next bubble is already forming, although which sector will be hit hardest remains to be seen.[131]

On August 1, 2011, Ron Paul opposed the so-called Budget Control Act of 2011 by stating:

> Rather than raising the debt limit, Congress should recognize the federal government has reached debt

saturation and therefore stop incurring new debt! Federal revenues for 2012 likely will amount to about $2.2 trillion, an amount roughly equal to the 2004 federal budget. To balance the 2012 budget, Congress simply needs to adopt 2004 spending levels. Was the federal government really too small just 8 years ago?

But Washington has a serious spending addiction—and in spite of all the talk about spending cuts, there are none contained in today's legislation. According to the non-partisan CATO Institute, this bill merely commits Congress to spending less than it otherwise would. Even if this Congress could bind a future congress, I doubt many Americans would define a cut as spending less on unconstitutional programs than Congress originally planned to spend. The bill also assumes large tax increases in its revenue projections, with the expiration of the Bush tax cuts at the end of 2012 calculated into the "baseline" numbers. This assumption will make it very difficult politically for Republicans to extend current tax rates beyond 2012.

Perhaps the most disturbing aspect of this deal is the "Super Congress" provision. This is nothing more than a way to disenfranchise the majority of Congress by denying them the chance for meaningful participation in the crucial areas of entitlement and tax reform. It cedes power to draft legislation to a special commission, hand-picked by the House and Senate leadership. The legislation produced by this commission will be fast-tracked, and Members will not have the opportunity to offer amendments. Approval of the recommendations of the "Super Congress" is tied to yet another debt ceiling increase. This guarantees that Members will face tremendous pressure to vote for whatever comes out of this commission—even if it includes tax increases. This provision is an excellent way to keep spending decisions out of the reach of members who are not on board with the leadership's agenda.[132]

Appendix: Warnings for the Future

On October 4, 2011, he said:

> Despite overwhelming grassroots support behind auditing the Fed, only incremental progress has been made toward unmasking the Federal Reserve's activities. Full transparency of the Fed's operations remains an elusive goal, but one towards which I intend to devote my remaining time in Congress....
>
> The Fed has been given a monopoly by Congress to conduct monetary policy, and in so doing it tinkers with the most important price of all, the rate of interest.... As we meet here in this hearing room, the Federal Reserve is engaging in the second coming of Operation Twist, attempting to force already-low interest rates even lower....
>
> With an official inflation rate of nearly four percent, interest rates on savings accounts of well less than one percent, and a stock market that has stagnated over the past three years, there is no incentive whatsoever for consumers to save or invest. Money sitting in the bank a year ago would have lost nearly four percent of its value by now, money invested in the stock market just as much, and money invested in Treasury bonds over one and a quarter percent. Is it any wonder that people have decided to consume rather than to save?
>
> Savings and investment are required for economic growth, deferring present consumption in the hopes of gaining some greater future consumption.... What the Federal Reserve's actions are telling people is: don't save, there is no need. ... Capital is being consumed through the government's spurring of consumption, encouraging people to take on debt to fund frivolous spending and failing not only to increase present capital but also failing to replenish capital that is used up in the production process.

This all leads us to the need for Federal Reserve transparency.... While the Federal Reserve is not fully transparent, what is transparent are the effects the Fed's policy actions have on everyday people. A young couple is thrilled that interest rates are at historic lows so they take out a mortgage in order to buy the house they had always wanted. But as the Fed continues to print money in order to suppress interest rates, the price of food and heating begins to rise. Expenses rise faster than their paycheck, and they find themselves falling behind on their mortgage and eventually face foreclosure.

Or imagine the elderly retiree dependent on Social Security and a small amount of savings. She has not received a cost of living increase to her Social Security in years, despite the ever-increasing cost of food and health care. Extended low interest rates mean that her savings account earns almost no interest each year, so her savings are rapidly depleting. She fears that within a couple of years she may be left with no money and no way to support herself.

And then there is the single mother who has been laid off from work for the past 18 months because the rising prices of production inputs caused by the Fed's inflationary monetary policy forced her employer to downsize the company in order to reduce costs. And with prices for the company's finished goods continuing to rise as the Fed continues pumping new money into the economy, consumer demand has dropped, making it all the more likely that her company will never be able to rehire her.

But rest assured, the Fed tells us, as long as the bankers are doing alright, everything will be fine. Indeed, the banks do appear to be doing fine. Flush with cash and receiving interest payments from the Fed on their excess reserves, the financial sector has continued to record amazing profits. Every time a new piece of disappointing economic data comes out, we hear renewed cries from

Appendix: Warnings for the Future

Wall Street for more action on the part of the Federal Reserve.

> Amazingly, some people are complaining that the latest round of $400 billion in bond purchases is too small. The fact that a $400 billion operation, equivalent to half the size of the Fed's pre-crisis balance sheet, is considered paltry is a sad indicator of how easily so many Americans are willing to accept big government. Bailouts of the financial sector are the new normal, only now they are conducted covertly through the Fed rather than through Congressional action so as not to arouse public ire as in 2008....
>
> Pumping trillions of dollars into the economy with no oversight and accountability cannot be allowed to continue. Audit the Fed now.[133]

On October 7, 2011, Ron Paul stated:

> While our domestic economy continues to suffer as a result of the Federal Reserve's intervention into credit markets, the euro increasingly looks likely to collapse. Here too the federal government has intervened, with the Federal Reserve promising unlimited dollar liquidity support to European central banks, and [Treasury] Secretary [Timothy] Geithner traveling to Europe to castigate the Europeans for moving "too slowly" in addressing their financial crisis....
>
> The Fed has not yet deigned to provide anyone with the details of these arrangements, so we have no idea how much money was promised or how this money will be used. Considering that swap lines peaked during the financial crisis at $580 billion, it would not be surprising to see that number reached or exceeded in the event that Europe faces a currency meltdown. It is imperative that we find out how much the US government has involved itself in negotiations surrounding the European financial crisis.[134]

In the *Wall Street Journal* on October 20, 2011, Ron Paul wrote:

> When central banks like the Fed manage money they are engaging in price fixing, which leads not to prosperity but to disaster.
>
> The Federal Reserve has caused every single boom and bust that has occurred in this country since the bank's creation in 1913....
>
> The great contribution of the Austrian school of economics to economic theory was in its description of this business cycle: the process of booms and busts, and their origins in monetary intervention by the government in cooperation with the banking system. Yet policy makers at the Federal Reserve still fail to understand the causes of our most recent financial crisis. So they find themselves unable to come up with an adequate solution.
>
> In many respects the governors of the Federal Reserve System and the members of the Federal Open Market Committee are like all other high-ranking powerful officials. Because they make decisions that profoundly affect the workings of the economy and because they have hundreds of bright economists working for them doing research and collecting data, they buy into the pretense of knowledge—the illusion that because they have all these resources at their fingertips they therefore have the ability to guide the economy as they see fit.
>
> Nothing could be further from the truth. No attitude could be more destructive. What the Austrian economists Ludwig von Mises and Friedrich Hayek victoriously asserted in the socialist calculation debate of the 1920s and 1930s—the notion that the marketplace, where people freely decide what they need and want to pay for, is the only effective way to allocate resources—may be obvious to many ordinary Americans. But it has not influenced government leaders today, who do not seem

Appendix: Warnings for the Future

to see the importance of prices to the functioning of a market economy....

> If the Fed would stop intervening and distorting the market, and would allow the functioning of a truly free market that deals with profit and loss, our economy could recover. The continued existence of an organization that can create trillions of dollars out of thin air to purchase financial assets and prop up a fundamentally insolvent banking system is a black mark on an economy that professes to be free.[135]

On November 30, 2011, he said:

> The Fed's latest actions in cooperating with foreign central banks to undertake liquidity swaps of dollars for foreign currencies is another reason why Congress needs enhanced power to oversee and audit the Fed. Under current law Congress cannot examine these types of agreements. Those who would argue that auditing the Fed or these agreements with central banks harms the Fed's independence should reevaluate the Fed's supposed independence when the Fed bails out Europe so soon after President Obama promised US assistance in resolving the euro crisis.

> Rather than calming markets, these arrangements should indicate just how frightened governments around the world are about the European financial crisis. Central banks are grasping at straws, hoping that flooding the world with money created out of thin air will somehow resolve a crisis caused by uncontrolled government spending and irresponsible debt issuance. Congress should not permit this type of open-ended commitment on the part of the Fed, a commitment which could easily run into the trillions of dollars. These dollar swaps are purely inflationary and will harm American consumers as much as any form of quantitative easing.

> The Fed is behaving much as it did during the 2008 financial crisis, only this time instead of bailing out politically well-connected too-big-to-fail firms it is bailing out profligate government spending. Citizens the world over deserve better than this. They deserve sound money that cannot be manipulated and created out of thin air by central planners who promise printed prosperity. Fiat money caused this European crisis and the financial crisis before it. More fiat money is not the cure. The global fiat currency system has proven itself a failure, we need real monetary reform. We need sound money.[136]

As the Congress convened to consider raising the debt ceiling yet again, on January 18, 2012, Ron Paul warned:

> Today the Congress is engaging in an act of futility. Despite the rhetoric on both sides, no one in Washington is truly interested in stopping the rising national debt. Some are wedded to trillions of dollars of welfare spending, while others treat the trillions of dollars of corporate welfare funneled to the military-industrial complex as absolutely sacrosanct. And so the national debt continues on its inexorable rise.
>
> If Congress were truly serious about stopping spending, it would have refused to raise the debt ceiling last summer. Instead, we were presented with a horrendous piece of legislation which gave the President his multi-trillion dollar debt limit increase with an incredibly high hurdle to stop the increase. Today's resolution of disapproval will unfortunately do nothing to stop the debt limit increase because there is no hope of passage in the Senate.
>
> Congress needs to get serious about cutting government spending. However, most proposed budget "cuts" are merely cuts to spending increases, not actually cuts from current levels of spending. If the federal budget can increase by hundreds of billions of dollars in a single year, there is no reason it shouldn't be able to decrease by hundreds of billions in a single year. Unless that happens

and Congress gets serious about reining in spending, the government will eventually have no choice but to default on its debt. Whether this is through outright debt repudiation or through the subtle and sinister method of inflation, the consequences will be painful for the American people.[137]

About the Author

Jeremy R. Hammond is an independent political analyst and recipient of the Project Censored 2010 Award for Outstanding Investigative Journalism. He is the founding editor of *Foreign Policy Journal* (www.foreignpolicyjournal.com) and can also be found on the web at www.jeremyrhammond.com.

While the study of economics initially held little interest for him, through his research and writing on matters relating to U.S. foreign policy, it became increasingly clear that the field of economics could not be separated from international affairs. While the U.S. government often publicly explained its actions in terms of such lofty ideals as defending "freedom", promoting "democracy" and "free trade", engaging in "humanitarian" military interventions, etc., it took only scratching the surface to realize that the rhetoric served to mask the true purposes for Washington's policies, which as a rule had everything to do with expanding U.S. power and influence, such as to open countries for the exploitation of their resources, prevent the emergence of competitors, and to maintain U.S. dollar hegemony as the world's reserve currency. There was perhaps no clearer example of this than the war on Iraq, which was sold under false pretexts, with the mainstream media doing its part to misinform the public by uncritically parroting official government lies.

Having already researched the Federal Reserve system and understanding how the Fed created "money" out of thin air at interest to the public (that is, how it is a debt-based monetary system), he had himself been warning that the U.S. economy was on an unsustainable course that must ultimately collapse. But when the financial crisis erupted in 2008, the housing bubble was nevertheless something of a mystery to him, with all the talk about "mortgage-backed securities", "derivatives", "toxic assets", etc. being something of a foreign language. He began studying the topic of economics even more earnestly in an effort to make sense of it all, and in doing so found that the explanations being offered by proponents of the Austrian school of economics—the ones who had actually predicted the crisis while most "experts" remained clueless—hands down made the most sense. And while most mainstream economists and financial pundits offered explanations consisting of more incomprehensible technical gibberish and newspeak, those of the Austrian school offered enlightenment on the subject in terms that most any non-economist could readily understand. In particular, he came to understand the role of the Fed's interest rate policy in causing the "business cycle" of artificial booms and their busts.

He discovered the website of Tom Woods (www.tomwoods.com), a senior fellow at the Ludwig von Mises Institute and bestselling author of numerous books (including *Meltdown*, which examines the financial crisis from a free-market perspective), who had compiled a useful and lengthy list of books and other materials available for free from the Institute's website (www.mises.org) and elsewhere for anyone interested in learning more about economics. In reading titles by Mises, Henry Hazlitt, Murray Rothbard, and other luminaries of the Austrian school whose work was refreshingly simple to understand, he found that not only was studying the topic not laborious, but such was the illumination offered by these writings that he actually found economics to be immensely (gasp) *interesting*. As his appetite for such knowledge grew, so also was magnified his understanding of his own particular focus, U.S. foreign policy.

In the aftermath of the financial crisis, he noticed with frustration how the free market was being blamed for what government intervention had caused, the narrative adopted by the mainstream media. He grew increasingly disturbed at how Ron Paul was dismissed as some kind of crackpot, even though he had accurately predicted the crisis, while Paul Krugman continued to be hailed as a genius, even though he had advocated the very same Fed policy that caused the housing bubble in the first place. *Ron Paul vs. Paul Krugman* is his own contribution to the effort to set the record straight.

Notes

[1] Ron Paul, "Other Dissenting View", Report of the House Banking Committee, "Housing Opportunity and Responsibility Act of 1997," April 25, 1997, http://web.archive.org/web/20040106035032/http://www.house.gov/paul/congrec/congrec97/dissent.htm. A number of the resources I draw on in this paper were included in a useful compilation of Krugman's remarks on the issue by Mark Thornton at the Ludwig von Mises Institute website, which I would like to gratefully acknowledge. See Mark Thornton, "Krugman Did Cause the Housing Bubble," Mises Economics Blog, Ludwig von Mises Institute, June 17, 2009, http://blog.mises.org/10153/krugman-did-cause-the-housing-bubble/. I'd also like to gratefully acknowledge the following websites as resources on Ron Paul's record: http://paul.house.gov/index.php?option=com_content&view=article&id=1007&Itemid=60, http://www.ronpaularchive.com/congressional-speeches-and-statements/, http://www.ronpaulsbrain.com. The latter in particular was helpful for providing a now inaccessible original source for his statements in earlier years, which, fortunately, may still be retrieved via the Internet Archive's Wayback Machine.

[2] Ron Paul, "Housing Opportunity and Responsibility Act of 1997," Statement on the Congressional Record, May 7, 1997, http://web.archive.org/web/20041114203139/http://www.house.gov/paul/congrec/congrec97/cr050797b.htm.

[3] Ron Paul, "Federal Reserve Has Monopoly Over Money and Credit in the United States," Statement on the Congressional Record, April 28, 1997, http://web.archive.org/web/20060602233708/http://www.house.gov/paul/congrec/congrec97/cr042897.htm.

[4] Paul Krugman, "Let's Not Panic – Yet," *New York Times*, August 30, 1998, http://www.nytimes.com/1998/08/30/opinion/let-s-not-panic-yet.html.

[5] Ron Paul, "A Worldwide Financial Crisis," Statement on the Congressional Record, Volume 144, Number 118, September 9, 1998, http://www.ronpaularchive.com/1998/09/a-worldwide-financial-crisis/.

[6] Ron Paul, "Worldwide Financial Crisis," Statement on the Congressional Record, Volumne 114, Number 119, September 10, 1998, http://www.gpo.gov/fdsys/pkg/CREC-1998-09-10/html/CREC-1998-09-10-pt1-PgH7555-6.htm.

[7] Ron Paul, "Revamping the Monetary System," Statement on the Congressional Record, Volume 114, Number 129, September 24, 1998, http://www.gpo.gov/fdsys/pkg/CREC-1998-09-24/html/CREC-1998-09-24-pt1-PgH8603-2.htm.

[8] Ron Paul, "World Financial Markets," Congressional Record, Page H9208, October 1, 1998, http://web.archive.org/web/20000916212259/http://www.house.gov/paul/congrec/congrec98/cr100198.htm.

[9] Paul Krugman, "The Capitalist; Dr. Mabuse Returns," *New York Times*, November 8, 1998, http://www.nytimes.com/1998/11/08/magazine/the-capitalist-dr-mabuse-returns.html.

[10] Ron Paul, "Hedge Fund Bailout," Congressional Record, Page E1894, October 2, 1998, http://web.archive.org/web/20090912032512/http://www.house.gov/paul/congrec/congrec98/cr100298.htm.

[11] Paul Krugman, "Money Can't Buy Happiness. Er, Can It?" *New York Times*, June 1, 1999, http://www.nytimes.com/1999/06/01/opinion/money-can-t-buy-happiness-er-can-it.html.

[12] Ron Paul, "Conference Report on S. 900, Gramm-Leach-Bliley Act," Congressional Record, Page E2297, November 8, 1999, http://web.archive.org/web/20100209062957/http://www.house.gov/paul/congrec/congrec99/cr110899-glb.htm.

[13] Paul Krugman, "A Leap in the Dark," *New York Times*, January 5, 2000, http://www.nytimes.com/2000/01/05/opinion/reckonings-a-leap-in-the-dark.html.

[14] Paul Krugman, "The Dishonest Truth," *New York Times*, February 23, 2000, http://www.nytimes.com/2000/02/23/opinion/reckonings-the-dishonest-truth.html.

[15] Paul Krugman, "Dow Wow, Dow Ow," *New York Times*, February 27, 2000, http://www.nytimes.com/2000/02/27/opinion/reckonings-dow-wow-dow-ow.html.

[16] Paul Krugman, "Reality Bites Again," *New York Times*, May 7, 2000, http://www.nytimes.com/2000/05/07/opinion/reckonings-reality-bites-again.html.

[17] Ron Paul, "Manipulating Interest Rates," Congressional Record, Page H3034, May 15, 2000, http://paul.house.gov/index.php?option=com_content&task=view&id=483&Itemid=60.

[18] Ron Paul, "Warning About Foreign Policy and Monetary Policy," Congressional Record, Page H9866, October 12, 2000, http://paul.house.gov/index.php?option=com_content&task=view&id=448&Itemid=60.

[19] Ron Paul, "Economic Problems Ahead," Congressional Record, Page H11866, November 13, 2000, http://paul.house.gov/index.php?option=com_content&task=view&id=441&Itemid=60.

[20] Paul Krugman, "Having A Banana?" *New York Times*, December 3, 2000, http://www.nytimes.com/2000/12/03/opinion/reckonings-having-a-banana.html.

Notes

[21] Ron Paul, "Economic Update," Congressional Record, Page H11939, December 4, 2000, http://paul.house.gov/index.php?option=com_content&task=view&id=438&Itemid=60.

[22] Paul Krugman, "We're Not Japan," *New York Times*, December 27, 2000, http://www.nytimes.com/2000/12/27/opinion/reckonings-we-re-not-japan.html.

[23] Paul Krugman, "Real Reality's Revenge," *New York Times*, December 31, 2000, www.nytimes.com/2000/12/31/opinion/reckonings-real-reality-s-revenge.html.

[24] Paul Krugman, "Herd on the Street," *New York Times*, January 3, 2001, http://www.nytimes.com/2001/01/03/opinion/reckonings-herd-on-the-street.html.

[25] Paul Krugman, "Secrets and Truths," *New York Times*, January 17, 2001, http://www.nytimes.com/2001/01/17/opinion/reckonings-secrets-and-truths.html.

[26] Ron Paul, "The Economy," Congressional Record, February 14, 2001, http://paul.house.gov/index.php?option=com_content&task=view&id=430&Itemid=60.

[27] Paul Krugman, "Will V Go To L," *New York Times*, February 25, 2001, http://www.nytimes.com/2001/02/25/opinion/reckonings-will-v-go-to-l.html.

[28] Paul Krugman, "Out of the Loop," *New York Times*, March 4, 2001, http://www.nytimes.com/2001/03/04/opinion/reckonings-out-of-the-loop.html.

[29] Paul Krugman, "Hangovers and Hang-Ups," *New York Times*, March 11, 2001, http://www.nytimes.com/2001/03/11/opinion/reckonings-hangovers-and-hang-ups.html.

[30] Paul Krugman, "After the Fall," *New York Times*, March 14, 2001, http://www.nytimes.com/2001/03/14/opinion/reckonings-after-the-fall.html.

[31] Paul Krugman, "Half a Loaf," *New York Times*, March 21, 2001, http://www.nytimes.com/2001/03/21/opinion/reckonings-half-a-loaf.html.

[32] Paul Krugman, "Dodging the Bullet," *New York Times*, May 2, 2001, http://www.nytimes.com/2001/05/02/opinion/reckonings-dodging-the-bullet.html.

[33] Paul Krugman, "Other People's Money," *New York Times*, July 18, 2001, http://www.nytimes.com/2001/07/18/opinion/reckonings-other-people-s-money.html.

[34] Interview with Paul Krugman, Lou Dobbs Moneyline, CNN, July 18, 2001, http://www.pkarchive.org/economy/ML071801.html.

[35] Paul Krugman, "Rebate and Switch," *New York Times*, July 29, 2001 http://www.nytimes.com/2001/07/29/opinion/reckonings-rebate-and-switch.html.

[36] Paul Krugman, "Blessed Are the Weak," *New York Times*, August 1, 2001, http://www.nytimes.com/2001/08/01/opinion/reckonings-blessed-are-the-weak.html.

[37] Paul Krugman, "Delusions of Prosperity," *New York Times*, August 14, 2001, www.nytimes.com/2001/08/14/opinion/reckonings-delusions-of-prosperity.html.

[38] Interview with Paul Krugman, Lou Dobbs Moneyline, CNN, August 22, 2001, http://www.pkarchive.org/economy/ML082201.html.

[39] Paul Krugman, "Greenspan Stands Alone," *New York Times*, August 31, 2001, www.nytimes.com/2001/08/31/opinion/reckonings-greenspan-stands-alone.html.

[40] Paul Krugman, "Hold Him To It," *New York Times*, September 9, 2001, http://www.nytimes.com/2001/09/09/opinion/reckonings-hold-him-to-it.html.

[41] Ron Paul, "The US Dollar and the World Economy," U.S. House of Representatives, September 6, 2001, http://paul.house.gov/index.php?option=com_content&task=view&id=393&Itemid=60.
[42] Paul Krugman, "After The Horror," *New York Times*, September 14, 2001, http://www.nytimes.com/2001/09/14/opinion/reckonings-after-the-horror.html.
[43] Frederic Bastiat, "That Which is Seen, and That Which is Not Seen," 1850, viewable online at http://mises.org/resources.aspx?Id=2735&html=1 and http://bastiat.org/en/twisatwins.html#broken_window. In brief, the fallacy lies in focusing on immediately seen effects while ignoring the unseen. The analogy is given of a shopkeeper's window being broken. This, according to the fallacious argument, will create economic growth because it creates a job for the glazier, who will in turn spend his earnings elsewhere into the economy, and so on. It's easy to see the job that was created by the destruction of his window, but what is *unseen* is how that same money would have been spent if the window had *not* been broken. The shopkeeper perhaps would have bought himself a new pair of shoes, and thus the shoemaker would have had a job and earned money to spend elsewhere into the economy. And the shopkeeper would thus have had shoes *and* a window. Thus, although it is true that a job was created for the glazier, there is no net benefit to the economy as a whole from the destruction of the window, but "Society loses the value of objects unnecessarily destroyed". If breaking windows could create wealth, we could encourage youths to cast rocks about and praise them for giving the economy a boost with their mischievousness.
[44] Paul Krugman, "Feat Itself," *New York Times Magazine*, September 30, 2001, http://www.nytimes.com/2001/09/30/magazine/fear-itself.html.
[45] Paul Krugman, "Fuzzy Math Returns," *New York Times*, October 7, 2001, http://www.nytimes.com/2001/10/07/opinion/reckonings-fuzzy-math-returns.html.
[46] Ron Paul, "Foolishness of Fiat," U.S. House of Representatives, October 31, 2001, http://paul.house.gov/index.php?option=com_content&task=view&id=381&Itemid=60.
[47] Paul Krugman, "Elven And Counting," *New York Times*, December 14, 2001, http://www.nytimes.com/2001/12/14/opinion/eleven-and-counting.html.
[48] Paul Krugman, "Could've Been Worse," *New York Times*, December 28, 2001, http://www.nytimes.com/2001/12/28/opinion/28KRUG.html.
[49] Paul Krugman, "The W Scenario," *New York Times*, February 22, 2002, http://www.nytimes.com/2002/02/22/opinion/the-w-scenario.html.
[50] Ron Paul, Statement before the House Financial Services Committee, Capital Markets Subcommittee, February 4, 2002, http://paul.house.gov/index.php?option=com_content&task=view&id=368&Itemid=60. Ron Paul, "Enron: Under-Regulated or Over-Subsidized?" *LewRockwell.com*, January 30, 2002, http://www.lewrockwell.com/orig/paul12.html.
[51] Ron Paul, "Economic Concerns, the Dangers Ahead, and Optimism…" U.S. House of Representatives, February 7, 2002, http://paul.house.gov/index.php?option=com_content&task=view&id=366&Itemid=60.

[52] Ron Paul, Statement on the Financial Services committee's "Views and Estimates for Fiscal Year 2003," U.S. House of Representatives, February 28, 2002, http://paul.house.gov/index.php?option=com_content&task=view&id=360&Itemid=60.

[53] Ron Paul, "Don't Expand Federal Deposit Insurance," U.S. House of Representatives, May 22, 2002, http://paul.house.gov/index.php?option=com_content&task=view&id=339&Itemid=60.

[54] Paul Krugman, "Where's The Boom?" *New York Times*, May 28, 2002, http://www.nytimes.com/2002/05/28/opinion/where-s-the-boom.html.

[55] Ron Paul, "Has Capitalism Failed?" U.S. House of Representatives, July 9, 2002, http://paul.house.gov/index.php?option=com_content&task=view&id=324&Itemid=60.

[56] Ron Paul, "The Free Housing Market Enhancement Act," U.S. House of Representatives, July 15, 2002, http://www.gpo.gov/fdsys/pkg/CREC-2002-07-15/html/CREC-2002-07-15-pt1-PgE1258-3.htm.

[57] Paul Krugman, "Living With Bears," *New York Times*, July 23, 2002, http://www.nytimes.com/2002/07/23/opinion/living-with-bears.html.

[58] Paul Krugman, "Dubya's Double Dip?" *New York Times*, August 2, 2002, http://www.nytimes.com/2002/08/02/opinion/dubya-s-double-dip.html.

[59] Paul Krugman, "Mind the Gap," *New York Times*, August 16, 2002, http://www.nytimes.com/2002/08/16/opinion/mind-the-gap.html

[60] Ron Paul, "Abolish the Federal Reserve," U.S. House of Representatives, September 10, 2002, http://paul.house.gov/index.php?option=com_content&task=view&id=313&Itemid=60.

[61] Paul Krugman, "The Vision Thing," *New York Times*, September 30, 2002, http://www.nytimes.com/2002/09/20/opinion/the-vision-thing.html.

[62] Paul Krugman, "Dealing With W," *New York Times*, October 1, 2002, http://www.nytimes.com/2002/10/01/opinion/dealing-with-w.html.

[63] Paul Krugman, "My Economic Plan," *New York Times*, October 4, 2002, http://www.nytimes.com/2002/10/04/opinion/my-economic-plan.html.

[64] Paul Krugman, "Lumps Of Coal," *New York Times*, December 27, 2002, http://www.nytimes.com/2002/12/27/opinion/lumps-of-coal.html.

[65] Paul Krugman, "Fear of a Quagmire?" *New York Times*, May 24, 2003, http://www.nytimes.com/2003/05/24/opinion/fear-of-a-quagmire.html.

[66] Paul Krugman, "Dropping The Bonds," *New York Times*, July 25, 2003, http://www.nytimes.com/2003/07/25/opinion/dropping-the-bonds.html.

[67] Paul Krugman, "Twilight Zone Economics," *New York Times*, August 15, 2003, http://www.nytimes.com/2003/08/15/opinion/twilight-zone-economics.html.

[68] Ron Paul, "Paper Money and Tyranny," U.S. House of Representatives, September 5, 2003, http://paul.house.gov/index.php?option=com_content&task=view&id=260&Itemid=60.

[69] Paul Krugman, "A Big Quarter," *New York Times*, October 31, 2003, http://www.nytimes.com/2003/10/31/opinion/a-big-quarter.html.
[70] Ron Paul, Statement on the Financial Services Committees "Views and Estimates for 2005", U.S. House of Representatives, February 26, 2004, http://paul.house.gov/index.php?option=com_content&task=view&id=247&Itemid=60.
[71] Ron Paul, "Government Spending – A Tax on the Middle Class," U.S. House of Representatives, July 8, 2004, http://paul.house.gov/index.php?option=com_content&task=view&id=232&Itemid=60. M3 is a measure of the total supply of money in circulation. The *Financial Times* explains: "M0 and M1, also called narrow money, normally include coins and notes in circulation and other money equivalents that are easily convertible into cash. M2 includes M1 plus short-term time deposits in banks and 24-hour money market funds. M3 includes M2 plus longer-term time deposits and money market funds with more than 24-hour maturity." See the Financial Times Lexicon: http://lexicon.ft.com/Term?term=m0,-m1,-m2,-m3,-m4. The Federal Reserve discontinued the disclosure of M3 in March 2006. For further information, see: "Discontinuance of M3," The Federal Reserve, November 10 2005, http://www.federalreserve.gov/releases/h6/discm3.htm. "The Money Supply," Federal Reserve Bank of New York, July 2008, http://www.ny.frb.org/aboutthefed/fedpoint/fed49.html.
[72] Ron Paul, "Raising the Debt Limit: A Disgrace," U.S. House of Representatives, November 18, 2004, http://paul.house.gov/index.php?option=com_content&task=view&id=220&Itemid=60.
[73] Paul Krugman, "A Whiff of Stagflation," *New York Times*, April 18, 2005, http://www.nytimes.com/2005/04/18/opinion/18krugman.html.
[74] Paul Krugman, "The Chinese Connection," *New York Times*, May 20, 2005, http://www.nytimes.com/2005/05/20/opinion/20krugman.html.
[75] Paul Krugman, "Running Out of Bubbles," *New York Times*, May 27, 2005, http://www.nytimes.com/2005/05/27/opinion/27krugman.html.
[76] Paul Krugman, "China Unpegs Itself," *New York Times*, July 22, 2005, http://www.nytimes.com/2005/07/22/opinion/22krugman.html.
[77] Paul Krugman, "That Hissing Sound," *New York Times*, August 8, 2005, http://www.nytimes.com/2005/08/08/opinion/08krugman.html.
[78] Paul Krugman, "Safe as Houses," *New York Times*, August 12, 2005, http://www.nytimes.com/2005/08/12/opinion/12krugman.html.
[79] Paul Krugman, "Greenspan and the Bubble," *New York Times*, August 29, 2005, http://www.nytimes.com/2005/08/29/opinion/29krugman.html.
[80] Paul Krugman, "Bernanke and the Bubble," *New York Times*, October 28, 2005, http://select.nytimes.com/2005/10/28/opinion/28krugman.html.
[81] Ron Paul, Statement on the Federal Housing Finance Reform Act of 2005, Congressional Record, Volume 151, Number 138, October 26, 2005, http://www.gpo.gov/fdsys/pkg/CREC-2005-10-26/html/CREC-2005-10-26-pt1-PgH9126-3.htm.

Notes

[82] Paul Krugman, "No Bubble Trouble?" *New York Times*, January 2, 2006, http://select.nytimes.com/2006/01/02/opinion/02krugman.html.
[83] Paul Krugman, "Debt and Denial," *New York Times*, February 13, 2006, http://select.nytimes.com/2006/02/13/opinion/13krugman.html.
[84] Ron Paul, "The End of Dollar Hegemony," U.S. House of Representatives, February 15, 2006, http://paul.house.gov/index.php?option=com_content&task=view&id=184&Itemid=60.
[85] Ron Paul, "What the Price of Gold is Telling Us," U.S. House of Representatives, April 25, 2006, http://paul.house.gov/index.php?option=com_content&task=view&id=178&Itemid=60.
[86] Paul Krugman, "The Phantom Menace," *New York Times*, June 16, 2006, http://www.nytimes.com/2006/06/16/opinion/16krugman.html.
[87] Paul Krugman, "Intimations of Recession," *New York Times*, August 7, 2006, http://www.nytimes.com/2006/08/07/opinion/07krugman.html.
[88] Paul Krugman, "Housing Gets Ugly," *New York Times*, August 25, 2006, http://www.nytimes.com/2006/08/25/opinion/25krugman.html.
[89] Paul Krugman, "Bursting Bubble Blues," *New York Times*, October 30, 2006, http://www.nytimes.com/2006/10/30/opinion/30krugman.html.
[90] Paul Krugman, "Credit Where Credit Is Due," The Conscience of a Liberal (Blog), *New York Times*, October 30, 2006, http://krugman.blogs.nytimes.com/2006/10/30/credit-where-credit-is-due/.
[91] Paul Krugman, "The Big Meltdown," *New York Times*, March 2, 2007, http://www.nytimes.com/2007/03/02/opinion/02krugman.html.
[92] Paul Krugman, "Just Say AAA," *New York Times*, July 2, 2007, http://www.nytimes.com/2007/07/02/opinion/02krugman.html.
[93] Mark A. Calabria, "Did Deregulation Cause the Financial Crisis?" Cato Policy Report, Vol. XXXI, No. 4, July/August 2009, http://www.cato.org/pubs/policy_report/v31n4/cpr31n4-1.pdf. Partnoy, Frank, How and Why Credit Rating Agencies are Not Like Other Gatekeepers. *Financial Gatekeepers: Can They Protect Investors?*, Yasuyuki Fuchita, Robert E. Litan, eds., Brookings Institution Press and the Nomura Institute of Capital Markets Research, 2006; San Diego Legal Studies Paper No. 07-46. Available at SSRN: http://ssrn.com/abstract=900257.
[94] Paul Krugman, "The Sum of Some Fears," *New York Times*, July 27, 2007, http://www.nytimes.com/2007/07/27/opinion/27krugman.html.
[95] Paul Krugman, "Very Scary Things," *New York Times*, August 10, 2007, http://www.nytimes.com/2007/08/10/opinion/10krugman.html.
[96] Paul Krugman, "Workouts, Not Bailouts," *New York Times*, August 17, 2007, http://www.nytimes.com/2007/08/17/opinion/17krugman.html.
[97] Paul Krugman, "It's a Miserable Life," *New York Times*, August 20, 2007, http://www.nytimes.com/2007/08/20/opinion/20krugman.html.
[98] Paul Krugman, "A Catastrophe Foretold," *New York Times*, October 26, 2007, http://www.nytimes.com/2007/10/26/opinion/26krugman.html.

[99] Paul Krugman, "Innovating Our Way to Financial Crisis," *New York Times*, December 3, 2007, http://www.nytimes.com/2007/12/03/opinion/03krugman.html.
[100] Paul Krugman, "Blindly Into the Bubble," *New York Times*, December 21, 2007, http://www.nytimes.com/2007/12/21/opinion/21krugman.html.
[101] Ron Paul, Statement before the Financial Services Committee, U.S. House of Representatives, September 20, 2007, http://paul.house.gov/index.php?option=com_content&task=view&id=142&Itemid=60.
[102] Ron Paul, Statement Before the Joint Economic Committee, U.S. House of Representatives, November 8, 2007, http://paul.house.gov/index.php?option=com_content&task=view&id=136&Itemid=60.
[103] Paul Krugman, "And I was on the grassy knoll, too," The Conscience of a Liberal (Blog), *New York Times*, June 17, 2009, http://krugman.blogs.nytimes.com/2009/06/17/and-i-was-on-the-grassy-knoll-too/.
[104] http://www.merriam-webster.com.
[105] Ibid., Comment #108, June 21, 2009. Interview with Paul Krugman, *Weekly Report* (Spain), May 2, 2009, http://www.rtve.es/alacarta/videos/informe-semanal/informe-semanal-innovar-para-salir-crisis/495712/. Krugman's reference was to the following piece of *satire*: "Recession-Plauged Nation Demands New Bubble To Invest In," *The Onion*, July 14, 2008, http://www.theonion.com/articles/recessionplagued-nation-demands-new-bubble-to-inve,2486/. Krugman, as seen, took the joke quite seriously.
[106] Paul Krugman, "How Did Economists Get It So Wrong?" *New York Times*, September 6, 2009, http://www.nytimes.com/2009/09/06/magazine/06Economic-t.html.
[107] Paul Krugman, "Me And The Bubble," *New York Times*, April 5, 2010, http://krugman.blogs.nytimes.com/2010/04/05/me-and-the-bubble/.
[108] Paul Krugman and Robin Wells, "The Slump Goes On: Why?" *The New York Review of Books*, September 30, 2010, http://www.nybooks.com/articles/archives/2010/sep/30/slump-goes-why.
[109] Paul Krugman, "The Worst Time to Slow the Economy," *New York Times*, July 9, 2011, http://www.nytimes.com/2011/07/10/opinion/sunday/10sun1.html.
[110] Paul Krugman, "The Wrong Worries," *New York Times*, August 4, 2011, http://www.nytimes.com/2011/08/05/opinion/the-wrong-worries.html.
[111] Paul Krugman, "Holding China to Account," *New York Times*, October 2, 2011, http://www.nytimes.com/2011/10/03/opinion/holding-china-to-account.html.
[112] Paul Krugman, "G.O.P. Monetary Madness," *New York Times*, December 15, 2011, http://www.nytimes.com/2011/12/16/opinion/gop-monetary-madness.html.
[113] Consumer Price Index News Release, U.S. Bureau of Labor Statistics, December 16, 2011, http://www.bls.gov/news.release/archives/cpi_12162011.htm.
[114] Paul Krugman, "Keynes Was Right," *New York Times*, December 29, 2011, http://www.nytimes.com/2011/12/30/opinion/keynes-was-right.html.
[115] Walter J. "John" Williams, "The Consumer Price Index", Part 4 of 5 of the article series "Government Economic Reports: Things You've Suspected But Were Afraid

to Ask!", October 1, 2006, http://www.shadowstats.com/article/consumer_price_index. See also John Williams' alternative inflation chart at http://www.shadowstats.com/alternate_data/inflation-charts.

[116] Henry Blodget, "Do You Realize That The Government Is Still Paying Banks Not To Lend...?" *Business Insider*, August 17, 2011, http://articles.businessinsider.com/2011-08-17/news/29985897_1_banks-financial-crisis-short-term-interest-rates.

[117] Paul Krugman, "Fake Me," The Conscience of a Liberal (Blog), *New York Times*, August 24, 2011, http://krugman.blogs.nytimes.com/2011/08/24/fake-me/.

[118] Budget and Economic Outlook: Fiscal Years 2011 To 2021, Congressional Budget Office, January 2011, http://www.cbo.gov/doc.cfm?index=12039.

[119] Ron Paul, Statement Before the Financial Services Committee Hearing, "Monetary Policy and the State of the Economy," U.S. House of Representatives, February 27, 2008, http://paul.house.gov/index.php?option=com_content&task=view&id=126&Itemid=60.

[120] Ron Paul, "Statement on HR 3221," U.S. House of Representatives, July 24, 2008, http://paul.house.gov/index.php?option=com_content&task=view&id=105&Itemid=60.

[121] Ron Paul, "Bailouts will lead to rough economic ride," CNN, September 23, 2008, http://edition.cnn.com/2008/POLITICS/09/23/paul.bailout/index.html.

[122] Ron Paul, Statement before the Joint Economic Committee, "The Economic Outlook," U.S. House of Representatives, September 24, 2008, http://paul.house.gov/index.php?option=com_content&task=view&id=97&Itemid=60.

[123] Ron Paul, Statement before the Financial Services Committee, Full Committee Hearing, "The Future of Financial Services: Exploring Solutions for the Market Crisis", September 24, 2008, http://paul.house.gov/index.php?option=com_content&task=view&id=96&Itemid=60.

[124] Ron Paul, Statement on the House Floor, "The Bailout," September 29, 2008, http://paul.house.gov/index.php?option=com_content&task=view&id=95&Itemid=60.

[125] Ron Paul, Statement of Congressman Ron Paul, United States House of Representatives, Statement on HR 1424, "The Passage of the Bailout," October 3, 2008, http://paul.house.gov/index.php?option=com_content&task=view&id=94&Itemid=60.

[126] Statement of Congressman Ron Paul, United States House of Representatives, "The Austrians Were Right," November 20, 2008, http://paul.house.gov/index.php?option=com_content&task=view&id=87&Itemid=60. On the Austrian economists predicting the Great Depression, for example, compare Milton Friedman's mentor Irving Fischer, who assured two days after the

peak of the bull market in 1929 that the turnaround in stock prices "will not be hastened by any anticipated crash, the possibility of which I fail to see" with F. A. Hayek, who warned of the impending crash of '29, saying "you cannot indefinitely maintain an inflationary boom. Such a boom creates all kinds of artificial jobs that might keep going for a fairly long time but sooner or later must collapse."

[127] Statement of Congressman Ron Paul, United States House of Representatives, "End the Fed," February 25, 2009, http://paul.house.gov/index.php?option=com_content&task=view&id=80&Itemid=60.

[128] Statement of Congressman Ron Paul, United States House of Representatives, "Introducing the Federal Reserve Transparency Act," February 26, 2009, http://paul.house.gov/index.php?option=com_content&task=view&id=78&Itemid=60.

[129] Chairman Ron Paul, Statement for the Record, Subcommittee on Domestic Monetary Policy, "Can Monetary Policy Really Create Jobs?" U.S. House of Representatives, February 9, 2011, http://paul.house.gov/index.php?option=com_content&task=view&id=1827&Itemid=60.

[130] Ron Paul, "Opening Statement on Hearing on Monetary Policy and the Debt Ceiling," U.S. House of Representatives, May 11, 2011, http://paul.house.gov/index.php?option=com_content&view=article&id=1007&Itemid=60.

[131] Ron Paul, "Statement on Impact of Monetary Policy on the Economy," U.S. House of Representatives, July 26, 2011, http://paul.house.gov/index.php?option=com_content&task=view&id=1899&Itemid=60.

[132] Ron Paul, "Statement on the Budget Control Act," U.S. House of Representatives, August 1, 2011, http://paul.house.gov/index.php?option=com_content&view=article&id=1007&Itemid=60.

[133] Ron Paul, Statement for the Record, United States House of Representatives, Committee on Financial Services, Subcommittee on Domestic Monetary Policy and Technology, Hearing on: "Audit the Fed: Dodd-Frank, QE3, and Federal Reserve Transparency," October 4, 2011, http://paul.house.gov/index.php?option=com_content&task=view&id=1916&Itemid=60.

[134] Ron Paul, Statement for the Record, Hearing to Receive the Testimony of the Secretary of the Treasury on the Annual Report of the Financial Stability Oversight Council, U.S. House of Representatives, October 7, 2011, http://paul.house.gov/index.php?option=com_content&task=view&id=1917&Itemid=60.

[135] Ron Paul, "Blame the Fed for the Financial Crisis," *Wall Street Journal*, October 20, 2011, http://online.wsj.com/article/SB10001424052970204346104576637290931614006.html.

Notes

[136] Ron Paul, Statement on the Fed's Continued Euro Bailout, U.S. House of Representatives, November 30, 2011, http://paul.house.gov/index.php?option=com_content&task=view&id=1931&Itemid=60.

[137] Ron Paul, Statement on the Debt Ceiling Disapproval Resolution, U.S. House of Representatives, January 18, 2012, http://paul.house.gov/index.php?option=com_content&task=view&id=1942&Itemid=60.

Index

9/11, 22, 44
austerity, 61
Austrian school of economics, 5, 14, 16, 17, 18, 58, 60, 66, 71, 82
bailouts, 8, 10, 24, 26, 28, 36, 41, 47, 65, 66, 68, 69, 70, 71, 73, 75, 81, 83
    Troubled Asset Relief Program (TARP), 69, 73
Bank of International Settlements, 72
Bastiat, Frederic, 22
Bernanke, Ben, 40, 45, 47, 58, 76, 77
bills. *See* Treasury Securities
bonds. *See* Treasury Securities
boom. *See* business cycle
bubble
    dot-com, 8, 10, 11, 13, 15, 20, 29, 30, 31, 32, 33, 39, 44, 45, 46, 47, 63, 77
    housing, 5, 16, 19, 20, 21, 23, 25, 26, 27, 28, 30, 31, 36, 37, 38, 39, 40, 41, 43, 45, 46, 47, 48, 49, 50, 53, 54, 55, 56, 57, 61, 63, 66, 67, 71, 77
Bush administration, 18, 40, 44
business cycle, 6, 7, 12, 13, 14, 16, 17, 18, 25, 31, 33, 35, 66, 67, 74, 82
bust. *See* business cycle

capitalism, 8, 12, 25, 27
CATO Institute, 78
China, 37, 38, 39, 40, 44
Clinton administration, 20
Congress, 8, 9, 11, 18, 20, 21, 22, 26, 29, 30, 35, 36, 37, 45, 65, 66, 67, 69, 70, 71, 72, 76, 77, 78, 79, 81, 83, 84, 85
    American Dream Downpayment Act, 50
    Budget Control Act of 2011, 77
    Community Reinvestment Act, 67
    Logan Act, 73
    Zero Downpayment Act, 50
consumer goods, 10, 15, 59, 60
Consumer Price Index (CPI), 15, 22, 59, 73
deficit
    trade, 44
deficit spending. *See* spending, government
deficits. *See* spending, government
deflation, 31, 33, 34
deregulation. *See* regulation
derivatives, 9, 48
Dobbs, Lou, 18, 19
dollar, 44
    as world reserve currency, 44
dollar, U.S., 9, 18, 20, 21, 24, 40, 44, 45, 57, 60, 69, 72, 73

as world reserve currency, 43, 44, 60
petrodollar system, 44
employment, 25, 32, 37, 38, 40, 44, 57, 61, 69, 73, 74, 75, 76
Enron, 25, 53
euro, 44, 45, 83
Europe, 81, 83
European Central Bank, 72
Export-Import Bank, 25
exports, 18, 46, 57, 60
Fannie Mae. *See* Goverment Sponsored Enterprises (GSEs)
Federal Deposit Insurance Corporation (FDIC), 9, 26, 70
Federal Open Market Committee, 76, 82
Federal Reserve, 7, 9, 10, 12, 13, 15, 16, 17, 18, 19, 20, 21, 22, 23, 24, 25, 26, 28, 29, 30, 31, 32, 33, 34, 35, 36, 37, 38, 39, 40, 43, 45, 46, 47, 48, 49, 50, 51, 53, 54, 55, 56, 57, 59, 61, 63, 65, 66, 69, 72, 73, 74, 75, 76, 79, 80, 81, 82, 83, 84
debt monetization, 20, 36, 40, 75, 76
Operation Twist, 79
quantitative easing, 73, 76, 77, 83
fiat currency, 8, 25, 36, 44, 45, 58, 84
financial crisis, 5, 6, 10, 12, 54, 66, 75, 84
Europe, 81
foreign policy, 43, 72
fractional-reserve banking, 60
Freddie Mac. *See* Government Sponsored Enterprises (GSEs)
free market, 5, 7, 15, 17, 21, 27, 40, 48, 49, 50, 60, 61, 67, 71, 82, 83
Geithner, Timothy, 81
General Motors, 73
gold, 44, 45

government debt. *See* spending, government
Government Sponsored Enterprises (GSEs), 10, 20, 21, 27, 29, 35, 40, 41, 50, 66, 67, 68, 70, 73
Great Depression, 22, 31, 58, 71
Greenspan, Alan, 9, 12, 16, 17, 18, 19, 23, 27, 29, 30, 33, 34, 40, 46, 47, 55, 77, 91
Hayek, Friedrich A., 5, 82
Hazlitt, Henry, 5
House of Representatives. *See* Congress
Housing and Urban Development Agency (HUD), 7
housing boom. *See* bubble, housing
Hussein, Saddam, 44
inflation, 7, 10, 12, 13, 15, 18, 22, 24, 27, 31, 36, 37, 43, 45, 57, 58, 59, 60, 72, 74, 75, 79
as a tax. *See* taxes, inflation as a tax
interest rates, 7, 8, 9, 10, 13, 16, 17, 18, 19, 22, 23, 24, 26, 29, 30, 31, 32, 33, 34, 35, 36, 37, 38, 39, 40, 43, 45, 47, 49, 53, 54, 55, 56, 60, 63, 74, 75, 76, 77, 79, 80
International Monetary Fund (IMF), 24
Iran, 44
Iraq, 44
Japan, 21, 23, 31
jobs. *See* employment
Keynes, John Maynard, 5, 17, 58, 61
Keynesian school of economics, 5, 17, 27, 37, 49, 58, 61, 71, 73
Krugman, Paul, 5, 6, 8, 9, 10, 11, 12, 13, 14, 15, 16, 17, 18, 19, 22, 23, 24, 26, 29, 30, 31, 32, 33, 34, 35, 37, 38, 39, 43, 45, 46, 47, 48,

Index

49, 53, 54, 55, 56, 57, 58, 59, 60, 61, 63
leverage, 9, 48
Long Term Capital Management LP, 9, 19
M3 money supply, 36, 45
malinvestment, 8, 12, 16, 22, 30, 33, 35, 66, 67, 72, 74, 75
McCulley, Paul, 29, 30, 38, 47
military industrial complex, 84
Mises, Ludwig von, 5, 82
Moody's. *See* rating agencies
moral hazard, 9, 11, 26, 48, 65, 68, 69, 70
Morgan Stanley, 29
mortgage, 21, 28, 34, 36, 40, 50, 56, 74, 80
  refinancing, 21, 32, 34, 37, 38, 46, 56
  subprime, 48
mortgage-backed securities, 10, 19, 21, 48, 49, 73
NASDAQ. *See* stock market
NASDAQ bubble. *See* bubble, dot-com
national debt, 37, 84, 85
New York Review of Books, 56
New York Times, 8, 53, 55
New York Times Magazine, 22
Nixon, Richard, 17, 27
Obama administration, 61, 83, 84
oil, 44, 45
Paul, Ron, 5, 6, 7, 8, 9, 10, 11, 12, 13, 14, 15, 16, 18, 19, 24, 25, 26, 27, 30, 31, 34, 35, 36, 37, 40, 41, 43, 45, 48, 50, 57, 58, 59, 60, 63, 65, 66, 67, 69, 71, 72, 75, 76, 77, 79, 81, 82, 83, 84
Pimco, 47
purchase of U.S. debt. *See* Treasury Securities
quantitative easing, 76
rating agencies, 48, 50

real estate bubble. *See* bubble, housing
recession, 13, 15, 16, 17, 18, 24, 25, 26, 29, 30, 31, 32, 33, 34, 35, 39, 46, 57, 63
regulation, 9, 47, 48, 49, 50, 68
Roach, Stephen, 29
Rothbard, Murray N., 5
Securities and Exchange Commission (SEC), 25, 48
ShadowStats.com. *See* Williams, John
Social Security, 80
spending
  consumer, 9, 16, 17, 19, 21, 22, 24, 29, 30, 32, 33, 34, 35, 37, 38, 43, 45, 46, 57, 71, 79
  government, 24, 25, 26, 35, 36, 37, 38, 43, 57, 75, 76, 77, 78, 83, 84
stagflation, 31, 37, 73
Standard & Poor's. *See* rating agencies
stimulus, 32, 61
stock market, 11, 12, 15, 19, 21, 23, 35, 79
stock market bubble. *See* bubble, dot-com
taxes, 36, 37
  inflation as a tax, 31, 36, 45
  tax cuts, 18, 30, 32, 33, 35, 78
  tax deduction, 21
  taxpayers, 9, 11, 24, 26, 29, 36, 40, 41, 47, 50, 65, 71, 77
taxpayers, 25
Treasury securities, 20, 21, 37, 38, 39, 68, 75, 76, 77, 79
U.S. Constitution, 72
U.S. State Department, 73
U.S. Treasuries, 44, 60, 71
unemployment. *See* employment
Venezuela, 44
Wall Street Journal, 82

weapons of mass destruction, 44   Williams, John, 59

Printed in Great Britain
by Amazon.co.uk, Ltd.,
Marston Gate.